Peter Monteath teaches history at Flinders University and writes about modern Australian and European history. He has a particular interest in German history and how over the last two centuries it has intersected with Australia. Wakefield Press published his collection of essays *Germans: Travellers, Settlers and Their Descendants in South Australia* in 2011.

Mandy Paul is Senior Curator, Exhibitions, Collections and Research at History SA. She has published on aspects of Australian cultural history, South Australian Aboriginal history and the intersection of history and law in native title practice, and is particularly interested in Indigenous history and South Australian social history. Her most recent exhibition is: *Interned: Torrens Island, 1914–1915*.

Rebecca Martin completed a Bachelor of Arts (majoring in history) and Laws (Hons) with a Diploma of Languages in German at the University of Adelaide in 2013. Rebecca currently works as an educator in the museum sector in Canberra and her interests include social history, military history and international law.

Peter Monteath
Mandy Paul
Rebecca Martin

Wakefield Press
16 Rose St
Mile End
South Australia 5031
www.wakefieldpress.com.au

First published 2014



Edited by Margot Lloyd, Wakefield Press
Designed and typeset by Rachel Harris, Bit Scribbly Design
Printing and quality control in China by Tingleman Pty Ltd

National Library of Australia Cataloguing-in-Publication entry

| | |
|---|---|
| Creator: | Monteath, Peter, author. |
| Title: | Interned: Torrens Island 1914–1915 / Peter Monteath, Mandy Paul and Rebecca Martin. |
| ISBN: | 978 1 74305 338 6 (paperback) |
| Notes: | Includes bibliographical references. |
| Subjects: | Bungardy, Frank – Diaries |
| | Dubotzky, Paul – Pictorial works. |
| | Torrens Island Internment Camp (S Aust.) – History |
| | Prisoners of war- – South Australia – Torrens Island – History |
| | Concentration camps – South Australia – Torrens Island – History |
| | World War, 1914-1918 – Concentration camps – South Australia – Torrens Island – History |
| Other Authors/ Contributors: | Paul, Mandy, author. Martin, Rebecca, author. |
| Dewey Number: | 940.317099423 |

Cover image: Ration distribution. Photograph by Paul Dubotzki.
State Library of New South Wales, MLMSS 261/2/17

If the reporter of the "Advertiser" or "Herald", two leading South Australian Newspapers had wendet his way on a fine afternoon to Torrens Island, and had taken the trouble to enquire about our treatment, he would have been astonished. He would have heard true complaints anough to fill a collum for a week of tru missery and sufferings, endured by Prisoners of War in their own land …

Frank Bungardy

# Contents

# Acknowledgements

This book and the exhibition it accompanies are the result of a fruitful partnership between Flinders University and History SA. This publication would not have been possible without the dedicated assistance of many individuals and institutions. First and foremost we are grateful to the Goethe Institute in Sydney, and in particular its director Dr Arpad Sölter, for making the book possible through a timely and generous financial contribution.

In our efforts to piece together the remarkably fragmented history of the Torrens Island camp we have been helped by many people in many places. In Adelaide the staff at the South Australian Archives Centre, the Barr Smith Library, the State Library of South Australia and the Army History Museum were cooperative beyond the call of duty. Special thanks to our colleagues at the Migration Museum, particularly Suzanne Redman. We would also like to express our thanks to Elspeth Grant, Rosa Garcia and Paul Longstaff, all of whom were able to point us to valuable sources. Fortunately, Adelaide is blessed with a number of individuals who placed a vast reservoir of knowledge of German-Australian history at our disposal. We owe a large debt of gratitude above all to Ian Harmstorf, Lyall Kupke, Mike Wohltmann and Lois Zweck.

Outside South Australia we have been aided by the staff at the State Library of New South Wales, the National Library of Australia and the Australian War Memorial. Among the historians at the Australian War Memorial Aaron Pegram offered helpful and gratefully received advice, as did Gerhard Fischer from the University of New South Wales, one of the pioneers in this field.

We drew inspiration from the work of Nadine Helmi, who has done more than anyone to highlight the rich photographic legacy of Paul Dubotzki. This is evident above all in the wonderful exhibition she curated on the internment camp at Trial Bay and in the book she wrote with Gerhard Fischer, *The Enemy at Home*. The reader – and viewer – of this book will soon discover that we, too, are deeply indebted to the late Paul Dubotzki and his achievements behind the shutter. If a picture is worth a thousand words, then Dubotzki left us many volumes on the troubled history of Torrens Island and the other 'German concentration camps' in the First World War. For this reason we are grateful to Dubotzki's descendant, Mr Dieter Kamper, for allowing us to reproduce the photographs, and also to Mr Franz Streibl, who played the crucial role in making those images available to us.

Thanks are due, too, to a number of others who generously provided us with images published here and displayed in the exhibition: the Australian War Memorial, the State Library of South Australia, the National Archives of Australia, the National Library of Australia, the State Library of New South Wales, the Cowgill family, Julie Tolley, the Broken Hill Historical Society, the South Australian Police Historical Society, History SA and Sydney Living Museums. Without their kind help, this book, and the exhibition which it accompanies, would have looked very different.

Finally we express our thanks and gratitude to Michael Bollen and his team at Wakefield Press, and designer Rachel Harris of Bit Scribbly Design, for converting a collection of texts and photographs into a book which, we all hope, will provide a lasting record of one easily neglected aspect of South Australia's experience of the Great War.

SS *Scharzfels* in Port Adelaide. After Australian authorities seized the Newcastle-built steamer as a 'prize of war' it was renamed *Araluen*. Sold to Japanese interests in 1924, the vessel then became the *Okuni Maru*. On 31 August 1944 it was sunk by a US submarine.

State Library of South Australia, B 41238

# 1. SS *Scharzfels*

When the SS *Scharzfels* steamed up South Australia's Gulf St Vincent early on the afternoon of 5 August 1914, there was one vital piece of information its German captain did not have at his disposal – only hours earlier, it had been announced that Australia was at war with Germany. *Scharzfels* had sailed from New York, but was flying a German flag. And on 5 August 1914, that was an enemy flag.

Under its own steam the vessel was piloted up the Port River and berthed. A customs officer boarded *Scharzfels* and instructed the master, Captain August Strycker, to haul down the flag. He also sealed the wireless apparatus, obtained the ship's papers and served a detention notice on the captain. While all that was happening, a naval guard of fourteen men boarded the vessel and kept an eagle eye on proceedings.[1] When the customs officers left, the naval guard remained. There was no way that *Scharzfels* was going to make good its flight under the cover of darkness, or indeed at any time.

The people of Adelaide had heard the news of the outbreak of war, but they were still coming to terms with it. If any event in Adelaide confirmed the reality of the war in those early days, it was the arrival of *Scharzfels*. Even as it was piloted into Port Adelaide, Union Jacks were being hoisted to the masthead of the Commercial Road flagstaff and on the staff of the town hall. The berthing at No 1 Quay was witnessed by a gathering of wharfies and other spectators, who took a keen interest in the unexpected appearance of the enemy in their midst. Within a couple of days, trains running to Port Adelaide and Largs Bay were crowded with naval and military men heavily laden with kitbags and rifles.[2]

The arrival of *Scharzfels* not only heralded the outbreak of war, it also posed a number of awkward questions. Above all, how were the cargo, the officers and the crew, indeed the vessel itself, to be treated?

After some legal wrangling the cargo was discharged. That happened first in Adelaide, then *Scharzfels* was allowed to head to Melbourne and Sydney, carrying the cargo destined for those ports. The vessel did so under Australian command with the original crew. The German captain and officers, however, were made to cool their heels in Adelaide.

With the cargo discharged, the crew returned to Adelaide but had to remain on board. It consisted of fifty-six 'coloured' Indian men, generally known at the time as 'Lascars'. Although they were British subjects, they were not permitted to land and so languished aboard *Scharzfels* until they could be transferred to a mail steamer and taken to Colombo.[3]

*Scharzfels* became the subject of legal disputation, the result of which was that a 'Prize Court' decided the ship could be claimed by the Australian Government as a war prize. The judgement was a matter of some controversy; its opponents complained bitterly that according to international law *Scharzfels*, its officers and crew should have been allowed to leave Australia. Instead, the vessel was renamed *Araluen*, and for the rest of the war and beyond plied Australian waters as part of the Commonwealth Government Line, flying an Australian flag.

As for the German captain, officers and engineers, a string of indignities awaited them. Soon after they were escorted from their vessel, they were taken to nearby Torrens Island, the location of a quarantine station where the unexpected guests could be accommodated. Within a couple of days of their arrest they gave the military authorities their parole. That is, they gave their word that they would not abscond or engage in any kind of belligerent activity; in return they would be permitted to live at liberty, providing they reported regularly to Australian authorities. For as long as Australia and Germany were at war – and in August 1914 no one could know how long that might be – they would not be permitted to leave the country for fear they might return home and join the Kaiser's military forces.

At the end of September Captain Strycker and his men were in suburban Adelaide at Keswick Barracks, the headquarters of the 4th Military District.[4] Just how long they were there and what transpired is not known. By early November some of them, at least, were living in a house in Semaphore. It must have been hugely frustrating for them, without work, thousands of kilometres from family and friends, and with no prospect of returning to their homeland in the foreseeable future.

At first Strycker and his men were a source of curiosity, but as the first months of the war rolled by, attitudes toward them hardened. It would be some time before Australian forces encountered Germans on the battlefields of Europe, but an image of the fearsome 'Hun' was already being created to persuade young Australian men to enlist and all other Australians to devote their energies to the war effort. In time, allegations of German atrocities on the battlefields of Belgium reached Australian shores. Fears grew that that the Kaiser had not just continental Europe but also the entire British Empire in his sights.

Captain Strycker and his men were better positioned than most to register this hardening of attitudes toward Germans. The Adelaide public was beginning to express its unease at their presence. As they were still living on parole, locals complained of their 'preferential treatment'.[5]

That unease turned to belligerence at a public meeting convened by the Mayor of Port Adelaide, Joseph Clouston, in mid-November 1914. The meeting vigorously protested at the officers 'being allowed to patrol the streets of Semaphore in the manner they were doing'. Presiding over an enthusiastic audience, 'including a number of ladies', Clouston delivered a simple message. The time had come, he insisted, when they should be prepared to fight 'those within as well as the foe without'. He had judged the mood perfectly, listening keenly as others proposed and endorsed the idea of forming a volunteer force of citizens who 'desired nothing from the Government except rifles and ammunition and officers to train them'. The motion passed resoundingly; the audience stood to sing the national anthem.[6]

The government could not mistake the mood, and in December the men from *Scharzfels* were moved from Semaphore, close to the Port, to the sleepy suburb of Magill 'on the grounds that the presence of the officers might lead to unpleasant scenes'.[7] But it would not stop there. The war was not over by Christmas, as the most sanguine had hoped, and when the new year began, anti-German sentiment plumbed new depths. On 7 April 1915 the 'favoured treatment' of Strycker and his men came to an end; they were returned to Torrens Island, location of an internment camp since October 1914. This time they joined hundreds of other 'enemy aliens' who had already been deprived of their liberty, and who were learning that life in the island's 'Concentration Camp' offered little joy.

THE COLISEUM
EUM
Rundle Street, A
LWIGG & SON
COLISEUM COLISEUM

# 2. German South Australia

Beehive Corner and Rundle Street around the turn of the century. Here and in the immediate vicinity were many signs of the German influence in Adelaide. Beehive Corner itself was the home of the German Carl Stratmann's confectionery business – bought by Haigh's in 1915 when Stratmann was forced out of business. It seems that Beehive Corner in the very early part of the war also housed the photographic studios of Paul Dubotzki, who would soon be interned on Torrens Island – and would take his camera with him.

State Library of South Australia, B 56370

If the men taken from *Scharzfels* chose to use the liberty they enjoyed on parole to explore Adelaide – as they probably did – they would have been struck by how familiar parts of it appeared. Even the most casual of visitors on a short stroll through central Adelaide might be struck by the town's German heritage.

From the railway station visitors would make their way past Parliament House, where for more than five decades German politicians had taken their places among governments and oppositions alike. In 1914 the attorney-general was Hermann Homburg, the principal of one of Adelaide's leading legal firms.

Not just in the country areas like the Adelaide Hills and the Barossa Valley, but in Adelaide itself there was a significant German presence. This image is of the German School in Wakefield Street in 1864; people are gathered for the annual parade and games.

State Library of South Australia, B 37440

At the western end of Rundle Street was Beehive Corner, premises of the German confectioner Carl Stratmann. Inside were two imposing figures of medieval German knights Stratmann had brought from his homeland. Heading east down Rundle Street, a visitor encountered a number of German businesses, among them Café Kindermann, where they might stop for a pastry named 'Berliner Pfannkuchen', or simply 'Berliner'. From the eastern end of Rundle Street it was a mere hop to the Botanical Garden, which owed a huge debt to its former director, the German Richard Schomburgk. He had laid out the gardens in a form still recognisable to this day, and it was Schomburgk who was responsible for the elegant glass Palm House, fully imported from Bremen and assembled on site piece-by-piece in 1877.

Just south of Rundle Street was Adelaide's so-called German Quarter. The main artery running through it was Wakefield Street, the address of such distinctively German institutions as the German Club and the Menz Biscuit Factory. The quarter housed pubs with a German character, among them the Tivoli, where German farmers

The German Consul-General, Dr Georg Irmer, and a welcoming party outside 'Detmold', the Hahndorf home of Alfred von Doussa, in 1907. The house is now called 'Hollydene'.

State Library of South Australia, B 30468

gathered on town visits. Three German churches – Bethlehem Church, located on the corner of Flinders Street and Sudholz Place, the Trinity Lutheran Church on Angas Street and St Stephen's on Wakefield Street – dwelt close to each other in sometimes fractious fraternity.

A glance at a map of South Australia in 1914 shows many a Teutonic-looking name. Adelaide itself was named for the German Princess Adelheid of Meiningen, who as Queen Adelaide became consort of the British monarch William IV. An eastern suburb was Klemzig, named for one of the Brandenburg villages left behind by some of the earliest German settlers in South Australia. Reaching further east into the Adelaide Hills and beyond were settlements with names including Hahndorf, Lobethal and Blumberg, while to the north-east in the Barossa Valley Germans had stamped their presence in Hoffnungsthal, Kaiserstuhl, Bethanien and Langmeil.

South Australia was indeed the most German of the Australian states. The proportion of its population which could claim either German birth or direct descent approached

10 per cent – higher than any other part of Australia. Moreover, the Germans had helped form the character of the colony from its very early years. The first significant numbers of Germans had arrived in 1838. They were 'Old Lutherans' fleeing religious persecution in Prussia, where the king was seeking to impose a unified state church, and with it a unified prayer book, on his subjects. Just at a time when the future of the colony seemed to hang in the balance, these Germans proved to be model settlers. They soon became renowned for their capacity to produce food for the fledgling settlement and to live in peace with their British neighbours.

Over the years that followed, different kinds of German settlers followed in the wake of those pious Old Lutherans. There were many whose motivation to emigrate was primarily economic. They responded to the promise of being able to exchange the poverty to which they seemed condemned in the Old World for material security, if not affluence, on the other side of the world. Land, they were told, was abundant, cheap, and above all fertile. South Australia offered the kind of future that appeared out of their reach at home.

Others were not so interested in land. They wanted to pursue their trades in a country that might value their skills and talents more than their German homelands did. Some responded to quite specific needs in the young colony, such as the miners from the Harz district of Hanover, who came to work in the fledgling mining industry in South Australia, an industry which was securing for the province a more stable economic footing.

Others came for political reasons. After the failure of Europe's democratic revolutions of 1848 and 1849, there were many disillusioned German liberals who sought not only to escape the threat of vengeful persecution at home but to play their part in the politically progressive context of Britain's bold South Australian experiment, a 'paradise of dissent'. Many such men and women of liberal persuasion were Berliners aboard the *Princess Louise*, a vessel which berthed in Port Adelaide in August 1849. Sooner or later, some of the entries on that vessel's passenger list – Schomburgk, Mücke, Bühring, Schramm, Linger, Basedow and others – would become household names in the colony.

It was just a few years after the arrival of the first wave of German migrants that German settlements were established in the Adelaide Hills. Other German settlers then pushed north into the Barossa Valley, and eventually east into the Murraylands, across the border into Victoria, as well as into the south-east. Others found their way to the mid-north or across to the Yorke and Eyre peninsulas. Indeed, most of South

Australia's Germans lived in rural areas, where over decades many preserved their language, their culture and their religion.

German immigration to South Australia waned in the last years of the nineteenth century. By that time, international circumstances had changed. Where earlier they had come from a patchwork of states, from Prussia or Hanover or Bavaria, they now hailed from a unified Germany. In 1871, under Prussia's 'Iron Chancellor' Otto von Bismarck, the map of Europe was redrawn, and at its centre was the German Reich. In time Germany would join the European scramble for colonies, claiming a number in Africa and the Pacific, and it would encourage its people to remain within the Empire. The flow of German settlers to Australia slowed. Nonetheless, by the early years of the twentieth century there were perhaps 100,000 German Australians, of whom about a third were born in one of the German states.[1]

There was much to admire about the contributions Germans had made to South Australia's history. Decades before the term 'multiculturalism' was invented, South Australia had provided something of a model of how it might work in practice. Across all fields of endeavour – economic, artistic, scientific, political, religious – Germans and their descendants were making worthy contributions. And they were generally well accepted by their non-German neighbours.

Yet it was not all peace and harmony; by the turn of the century, strains in the relationship between British and German South Australians were beginning to show. Their causes lay not so much in South Australia but in other parts of the world. When the Boer War broke out in 1899, the Kaiser made his support for the Boers known, incurring the wrath of many Britons. South Australia for its part stood solidly behind Britain and sent forces to South Africa to fight the Boers.

Like the creation of a unified Germany, Australia's own unification in the form of Federation in 1901 brought with it a wave of nationalist sentiment. South Australia was no longer a colony but a state within the newly established Australian Commonwealth. As in any process of nation-building, questions arose about who belonged to this new nation, and who did not.

South Australia's Germans generally thought of themselves as loyal Australians. Most had no reason to feel an attachment to a state on the other side of the world which might not have even existed when they or their forebears came to South Australia. Indeed, there were some who thought that they were more devoted 'South Australians' than their British counterparts. Germans, after all, had come to South

Vineyard, Nuriootpa c.1900

Courtesy Julie Tolley

Australia in the first place precisely because they had chosen to build new lives outside Germany. The same could not be said of their British neighbours, many of whom found comfort in the notion that their adoptive homeland was a replica of Britain, if not simply an extension of it.

Whatever protestations South Australia's Germans might make in the first years of the twentieth century, the loyalty issue would not go away. The Boer War might have ended, but international tensions between Britain and Germany remained. Especially among recent immigrants, there were some Germans who expressed a strong emotional attachment to the united Germany they had left behind. Most of South Australia's Germans, however, saw no anomaly in cultivating a love of German culture, while professing an unswerving political allegiance to Australia. Their critics, nonetheless, remained convinced that only those who broke with their German roots and embraced Britishness in all its forms could be truly loyal to Australia.

With the outbreak of war in 1914, the ultimate test of loyalty was set. From the very beginning, South Australia's Germans moved quickly to provide a clear statement of their loyalty to Australia. As early as 4 August the elected president of the Evangelical Lutheran Synod in Australia of Eudunda, Pastor Theodor Nickel, sent a telegram to the Governor-General, Sir Ronald Munro-Ferguson. He told him, 'Although we deeply deplore that Great Britain has been involved in the European conflict and has been impelled to declare war on Germany, the land of our fathers, we are well aware of our duty as British subjects and shall always be willing to defend the honour of our beloved King and our dear country with goods and chattels, and body and life.' The Governor-General offered a gracious acknowledgement, stating that he was 'deeply gratified and touched by your message of loyal devotion to King and his Majesty's words: united, calm, resolute, trusting in God. Ferguson. Gov. Gen.'[2]

Those cordial mutual assurances would receive their first test the very next day, when *Scharzfels* appeared on Adelaide's horizon. Many more tests would follow in the next four years, and they would not always be dealt with so graciously.

# 3. Interned

Outnumbered! A photograph by Paul Dubotzki records the arrival of a prisoner on the island. Dubotzki's caption on the back reads, 'In 1914/1915 no German was brought in with fewer than ten guards'.

National Library of Australia 5016753

## South Australia at war

Reports in Adelaide newspapers of the assassination of Archduke Franz Ferdinand and his consort in Sarajevo on 28 June 1914 focused on the resulting 'universal sorrow' in Europe and the impact of the events on the elderly Franz Josef, Emperor of Austria and King of Hungary.[1] At the time, there was no indication that this would be the first step towards a war which would engulf Europe and draw in Europe's empires across the globe.

Australia was in the midst of an election campaign, with the election date set for 5 September. Caretaker Liberal Prime Minister Joseph Cook and Labor Leader of the Opposition Andrew Fisher were touring the country, but it was only after Austria-Hungary declared war on Serbia on 28 July, a month after the assassination in Sarajevo, that events in Europe began to feature in the campaign.[2]

Fisher arrived in Adelaide on Wednesday 29 July, taking lunch at Parliament House and afternoon tea at Trades Hall. That evening he addressed an enthusiastic audience at a packed meeting at the Exhibition Building. His only reference to war was in passing, and in the context of contrasting Labor policy of paying for defence (out of revenue) with that of the Cook government, which was seeking loans to present a Dreadnought to Britain. Labor, he promised, 'would send the last man and the last shilling against an armed foe'.[3]

Readers of the morning *Advertiser* opened their papers on Friday 31 July to a thoughtful editorial headed 'The State of Europe'. It mused on the fact that 'while the Powers are still negotiating with a view to peace their legions are buckling on their armour and steadily, if slowly, massing'. Yet the Triple Alliance and the Triple Entente had 'been lauded for years as the great twin pillars on which the peace of Europe rests', based on the fact that 'no single Power could move against any other without involving all Europe in universal and devastating conflict'. This was the guarantee against a policy of adventure – 'so it seemed to everyone'.[4]

As daily developments in Europe made war seem more likely, pledges of loyalty and support for Great Britain and 'the Empire' came from the leaders of both the government and opposition. Campaigning in Horsham, Victoria, on 31 July, Cook left no room for doubt: if war was to break out in Europe, 'all our resources in Australia are in the Empire and for the Empire, and for the preservation and security of the Empire'.[5] Fisher, speaking on the same day in Colac, Victoria, reprised the phrase he used in Adelaide to declare:

> All, I am sure, will regret the critical position existing at the present time, and pray that a disastrous war may be averted. But should the worst happen after everything has been done that honour will permit, Australia will stand beside our own to help and defend her to our last man and last shilling.[6]

On the first day of August, Germany declared war on Russia. On 3 August, Germany declared war on France.

At a special meeting in Melbourne on that day, the federal Cabinet decided to 'place the vessels of the Australian Navy under the control of the Admiralty'. And following the lead of Canada and New Zealand, the Australian Government offered to raise and fund an expeditionary force of 20,000 men to be sent 'to any destination desired by the Home Government'. Fisher had been consulted about this offer and confirmed his support.[7]

The question of the loyalty of German South Australians was already being asked, and answered. On the night of 3 August, members of the South Australian House of Assembly Friedrich Pflaum and Attorney-General Hermann Homburg spoke at a meeting of the Liberal Union held at Murray Bridge. A report of the meeting noted that they were both 'Germans' and continued:

> Mr Pflaum said that the question had been asked what Germans in South Australia would do in the event of Great Britain becoming involved in war with Germany. He said, 'I will tell them that, in such a case, the Germans who have lived under, and enjoyed the privileges of, the British flag, will go with their fellow Australians, and stand shoulder to shoulder with them to retain this beautiful land as a pearl in the British crown.'

German Club, Adelaide, 1914.

History SA, South Australian Government Photographic Collection GN 05182

This was 'received with tremendous enthusiasm', and Homburg later endorsed Pflaum's 'every word', saying he had 'beautifully expressed the position'.[8]

The South Australian Parliament sat the following day. Premier Archibald Peake reported to the House of Assembly that he had sent the Prime Minister a telegram expressing the 'keen satisfaction' of his government 'at the action taken by your Government in offering navy and men to the Motherland' and that 'this State will heartily co-operate with the Federal Government for the good of the Empire'.[9]

Peake noted that South Australia had been 'caught by the outer edge of a tremendous maelstrom in which the great nations of the world have become deeply involved' and spoke of his belief that people would unite in these changed circumstances. He also noted that 'we are a mixed community' and cautioned against the danger posed by the 'awakening' of racial animosities. In deploring this possibility, he said:

> I hope that it will be borne in mind that we are all fellow-citizens, and that the loyalty of South Australians, no matter from what stock they may have come, is thorough and undoubted.

Before the House adjourned, members, those in the public galleries and the press rose in their seats and sang the national anthem with enthusiasm. Three ringing cheers were given for the King.[10]

On the other side of the globe, German troops invaded Belgium.

The British Empire was at war with Germany from 11 pm London time on 4 August. In Australia, Governor-General Ferguson received the news by cable at 12.30 pm on 5 August. He, in turn, informed Prime Minister Cook and the state governors. At about 12.45 pm, Cook passed on the news to the papers, announcing: 'Australia is now at war'.[11]

In South Australia, parliament met at 2 pm, ministers sporting miniature Union Jacks on their lapels.[12] Premier Peake announced he had received a message from the Prime Minister that 'Official information has been received that hostilities have commenced between Great Britain and Germany'. Parliament also received a message from Governor Sir Henry Galway: 'I pray that with God's help South Australia may be guided safely through the crisis into which our Empire has been drawn'.[13]

That morning the Governor had received Mr Hugo Muecke, the German consul, the purpose of whose visit was to: 'explain that his position [as consul] did not in any

way affect his good and loyal citizenship in this State'. He was courteously received by the Governor and his assurances of loyalty readily accepted.[14]

People gathered outside government offices, Victoria Square, Adelaide, following the announcement of war on 5 August 1914.

History SA, South Australian Government Photographic Collection GN 01360

News the British Empire was at war travelled quickly. At five o'clock that afternoon there was a 'patriotic demonstration' outside the government offices in Victoria Square. Organised by public servants, the gathering began with the Adelaide Police Band playing 'The Song of Australia' – accompanied enthusiastically by the growing crowd. Three cheers were given for the King, the British navy and the allies of Great Britain. A message from the Governor was read, which concluded with a request that the people of South Australia 'keep a stiff upper lip'. The band followed with the national anthem and, at the request of someone in the crowd, 'La Marseillaise'.

Lastly, the thousands-strong crowd joined the band in a spirited rendition of 'Rule Britannia'. Flags featured, as the *Advertiser* reported:

> There was a spontaneous outburst of cheering when a large Union Jack was hoisted from an office window near the band. Smaller flags seemed to spring up simultaneously in various parts of the crowd, and these were waved to and fro by the holders until the ceremony was concluded.

The reporter suggested that the flying of the Union Jack symbolised the 'deep affection of the Dominions which were ready to sacrifice everything' for Britain.[15]

The newspaper reported similar scenes in towns around South Australia. In Kapunda,

> The news that England had declared war was received with silence at first, and then a flag of the Empire was unfurled in front of the Post-Office. A crowd joined in singing the National Anthem, Sons of the Sea, and Rule Britannia, winding up by prolonged cheers for King George.[16]

The mobilisation of South Australian infantry, artillery, army medical corps and naval reserves started on the afternoon of 5 August.[17]

The following day's *Register* included an editorial headed 'Fair Play, Britons!'. Referring back to the pledges of loyalty made by Pflaum and Homburg, 'prominent and esteemed State legislators of German descent', it exhorted 'Britons' to 'be generous and fair and big-minded and big-hearted in their relations with men and women of German extraction in this community'; to 'play the game as they would like the game to be played with them in similar circumstances'.[18]

## The enemy within

On Monday 10 August, five days after the announcement that Australia was at war, a proclamation was issued calling upon German subjects to report themselves to the police station nearest to their residences. On 12 August, war was declared against Austria, and the following day the measure was extended to Austrian subjects.[19]

The process of registration at the police station involved the completion of a form which included personal details, length of residence in Australia, naturalisation details and nationality, whether a member of the armed forces or reserves of an enemy country, possession of any firearms, as well as the names of 'reputable persons' to whom the person registering was known. Those being registered were asked to give their 'parole', to swear that they would 'neither directly nor indirectly take any action prejudicial to the British Empire during the present war'. The police officer could then make a 'provisional order', stating any requirements, such as reporting at the police station at stated intervals (usually weekly). The officer was then required to complete a confidential 'Report on Person reputed to be an Enemy Subject', which was filed with military intelligence.[20]

Photograph by Paul Dubotzki of the first camp on Torrens Island in early 1915. Opened in October 1914, the first camp was located just south of the existing quarantine station. The Port River, with sailing boat, is visible in the background. Accommodation was in tents; the rough wooden structures served as crude camp kitchens. Soon after this photo was taken, the site of the camp was moved to the southern end of the island, near where the Torrens island power station is now located.

Dubotzki Collection, courtesy Dieter Kamper

The Australian Government detained enemy aliens using discretionary powers delegated by the Imperial Government. Enemy reservists were a source of particular concern. Instructions from London, received on 7 August, required the arrest of enemy reservists in Australia. Most were then released on parole. In September further instructions were received stating that all enemy reservists and enemy subjects of military age found on ships should be detained. The following month the regime was extended: all enemy subjects whose conduct was considered 'suspicious or unsatisfactory' were to be interned. In December 1914 the Australian Government adopted the practice being followed in the United Kingdom of treating all internees, civilian or otherwise, as prisoners of war. From this point no distinction in terms of treatment or terminology was made between interned enemy reservists, enemy civilians, and interned British subjects: they all became 'prisoners of war'.[21]

These instructions received from Britain between August and October necessitated the establishment of internment camps in each military district. In South Australia, the 4th Military District, an internment camp was established on Torrens Island. In both common and official usage, and following British practice in the Boer War, it quickly became known as Torrens Island Concentration Camp.

Initially, those interned at Torrens Island after it opened on 9 October 1914 were enemy reservists and those of military age taken from ships, and enemy subjects whose conduct was considered 'suspicious or unsatisfactory'. Even before the camp's establishment, by the end of September 1914 over 50 men had been refused parole or taken off ships in South Australia. By the end of October, the number of internees held on Torrens Island was just under 100, and just under 200 by the end of 1914. Internments at Torrens Island continued until mid-August 1915.

Government records were kept of those interned; however, the records are incomplete, and there are inconsistencies between those records kept in South Australia in the first year of the war and those created later. There is enough information in the archives, however, to draw some general conclusions about who was interned at Torrens Island and why.

About 30 sailors and ships' officers were interned on Torrens Island; the steamship *Scharzfels* was only the first ship to lose crew members. The barque *Kilmallie* arrived in Port Adelaide from Santos, Brazil, on 5 December 1914, and six members of the ship's crew of military age, all German subjects, soon found themselves interned at Torrens Island.[22]

Internment and internment camps were topics subject to censorship. Although the first Deputy Chief Censor was appointed on 3 August 1914, it took some months to establish the mechanisms and limits of censorship in Australia. Once censorship was operational, newspapers were not permitted to refer to internment, and any material relating to the internment camps had to be submitted to the censor before publication.[23] The arrival of the *Kilmallie* was reported in the 'Shipping News'; no news was published relating to the internment of the six crew.

Early in the war, most of those interned were men who had been refused parole. About a quarter of Torrens Island internees fell into this category. As the war wore on, some of those who had given their parole failed to comply with its terms: about one third of those on Torrens Island had 'not complying with parole' marked alongside their names on the nominal roll. It is not recorded whether these men failed to comply with an administrative condition (such as reporting to a particular police station each week) or whether their lack of compliance was more substantive, relating to their undertaking not to take any actions prejudicial to the British Empire during the war. However, a handful of internees had 'failed to report' recorded, and about the same number 'acting disloyally' or 'making disloyal utterances'. A small number of men were interned because they refused to swear parole.

The federal election on 5 September resulted in a decisive victory for Labor. On 17 September 1914 the new government was sworn in, with Fisher as Prime Minister and William ('Billy') Hughes as Attorney-General. The government went about putting Australia on a war footing. The *War Precautions Act* was proclaimed on 29 October 1914, and its first regulations two days later. Among the wide wartime powers gained by the Australian Government under this Act was the power to intern naturalised British subjects – that is, its own citizens. Paragraph 26 of the regulations gave the Minister for Defence the power to detain by warrant any naturalised person whom the minister had 'reason to believe' was 'disaffected or disloyal'.[24]

For the decade before the war, the process of naturalisation in Australia was relatively simple: after two years of residence, the applicant completed a form and signed an oath of allegiance. A certificate of naturalisation arrived in the post some weeks later. But becoming a 'naturalised British subject' did not necessarily mean relinquishing original nationality – German, for example – and, after October 1914, naturalisation neither offered any legal protection against internment nor was seen as evidence of loyalty.[25]

Fewer than ten of those interned at Torrens Island were naturalised British subjects. Of these, three were noted as 'naturalised disloyal'. A further four naturalised British subjects held on Torrens Island were 'de-naturalised' during the course of the war, and three of these men were repatriated at war's end. This is consistent with the pattern Australia-wide; the power to intern naturalised British subjects was used sparingly.[26]

The South Australian election of March 1915 provided a barometer of the change in attitudes towards the state's German population. It brought not just a change of mood but a change of government. The former attorney-general, the Norwood-born Hermann Homburg, was forced to resign in January of that year; his office had been raided by soldiers with fixed bayonets the previous year. When he stood for re-election in March, he lost, as did other candidates with German names. Among those defeated was the premier, Archibald Peake, who was known to harbour some sympathies for the state's Germans; the anti-German vote appears to have been a significant factor in the change of government.[27]

Internments at Torrens Island continued steadily, with monthly arrivals peaking at more than 50 in January 1915. The rate of internment then declined, with one or two dozen men taken to Torrens Island most months. The exception was May 1915, with over 40 new internments. In the same month, the Bryce Report was released. This report, the work of a British parliamentary committee inquiring into allegations of German atrocities on the Western Front, led to a hardening of British and Australian attitudes to Germans. Earlier anti-German sentiment had been directed primarily at the Kaiser or at an abstract notion of 'Prussian militarism'. But with the appearance of the Bryce Report, as one historian has put it, 'friend turned upon friend and mate upon mate. The Bryce committee's document ensured that anti-German feelings would be personalised'.[28]

Also in May 1915, the concept of the enemy within was widened to include 'natural-born' British subjects, that is, people born in Australia of German or Austro-Hungarian descent. Under new *War Precautions Act* regulations, a paragraph was added, No. 56: if the minister had any reason to believe 'any natural-born British subject one at least of whose parents was or is a subject of a State which is at war with the King, is disaffected or disloyal, he may, by warrant under his hand, order him to be detained in military custody . . .'[29]

No natural-born British citizens of German or Austrian descent were interned at Torrens Island. This was consistent with the timing of the introduction of this provision (only three months before the closure of Torrens Island) and the generally cautious use of this potentially politically difficult power.[30] Eventually, as we shall see, a number of individuals of German descent born in South Australia would find themselves interned in New South Wales.

It was not only enemy subjects who were sailors and reservists, or who broke parole, or were 'disaffected or disloyal', who found themselves interned on Torrens Island. Some men surrendered for voluntary internment.

The combination of the onset of war, economic downturn (particularly in the mining industry), the exclusion of enemy subjects from maritime occupations, and the rise of anti-German feeling, including among trade unions, left many enemy subjects resident in Australia without work, and unable to access any form of employment relief. Voluntary internment provided a solution.[31]

Destitute enemy subjects could give themselves up for voluntary internment from early in the war. For the period that the Torrens Island internment camp was operating, voluntary internees could be released from internment if they could show that they had secured employment. While the patchy nature of records makes accurate assessments of the number of voluntary internees difficult, it appears that slightly more than one in ten Torrens Island internees fell into this category.[32]

All of the internees in the Torrens Island camp were men, but women and children, too, were deeply affected by internment. The prolonged absence of men, and especially of breadwinners, could cause great hardship. The Commonwealth Government provided an allowance to families of internees, both voluntary and involuntary, based on the rate of the other Commonwealth pensions of the period, the aged and invalid pensions. The allowance was 10 shillings per week, plus two

Once a Hun, always a Hun. By 1915 more reports of alleged German atrocities were appearing in the Australian press. The Australian Government used images of the horrible Hun to promote enlistment in the AIF. This recruitment poster was produced by the Government Printer in 1915.

State Library of New South Wales a184021

shillings and sixpence for each child under 15, for a maximum of three children. The rate was increased to 12 and six in 1916.[33] Many families found the allowance inadequate.

Internee Frank Bungardy wrote in his diary of a woman put in this difficult position because the government of the land of her husband's birth 'is at loggerheads with the government of the land of his adoption'. He later wrote of the allowance received by his wife:

> I look upon this amount as a starvation allowance, especially with the high prices ruling for foodstuff . . . I consider the amount granted, by the Military authoritys insufficient to pay for the comodities to keep body and soul together, especially as the head of the family and Breadwinner has been forcibly been taken away from them and keept in idlenes and so unable to earn any money, wich would help his distant family along, at least to a certain extent. I have often pittied the poor australian Women who wher unfortunately married to an Enemy subject, also the offsprings of such a marriage. I am positive the Larder of these unfortunate Mother has been empty on many occasion during the European struggle . . .[34]

The 'poor Australian woman' imagined by Bungardy would, by virtue of taking her husband's nationality on her marriage, have herself been an enemy subject.[35] Aside from this technicality, she may have found the anti-German feeling responsible for her economic circumstances extended to her family.

Internment in South Australia effectively finished in mid-August 1915, when the Torrens Island internment camp was closed and most of the prisoners transferred to Holsworthy, near Liverpool, in New South Wales.

About 400 men spent time interned on Torrens Island in the ten months it operated. Of those, the overwhelming majority (almost 350) were German subjects. While many of those men had lived and worked for years in South Australia, others were short-term residents or visitors. Of the remaining internees, there were a few more than twenty from Austria-Hungary, and a sole representative from Turkey, who is entered on the nominal roll under the name Sulaman Mustala. Fewer than ten internees were naturalised British subjects, and none of those held on Torrens Island were natural-born (Australian) British subjects of enemy descent. It was not surprising, then, that the camp on Torrens Island was referred to as the 'German Concentration Camp'.

# The Bavarian Band

The German Club Band, 1906. This band shared some of its members with the Bavarian Band. The cellist fourth from the left in the middle row is probably Ludwig Reinheimer, who in 1919 surrendered for repatriation to Germany.

Courtesy Carolyn Cowgill

Well known around Adelaide on the eve of the war was the Bavarian Band. When some of the band's members failed to report weekly to the military authorities as required, they were arrested and taken to Keswick Barracks. The next morning, 15 January 1915, five band members were escorted to bandmaster Henry Wirth's Peel Street home, where they had been residing. They were given the opportunity to quietly collect their belongings before internment on Torrens Island; their presence in town under military guard attracted quite a crowd.

Henry Wirth was reportedly the only member of the band with a wife in Australia. Mrs Wirth was 'visibly distressed' at her husband's internment, but she might have drawn some consolation from words published the next day in the *Daily Herald*:

> In all probability it has been a kindness to the Bavarians to place them where they will not be allowed to starve, for during the past few weeks they have not been able to make a living in the streets, although they have churned out the martial strains of 'Tipperary' until even the German instruments must feel the strain on their capacity and 'kultur'.

## Broken Hill

The German Club House in Broken Hill, New South Wales, after an arson attack in January 1915.

Courtesy Broken Hill Historical Society

On New Year's Day in 1915 two men shot dead four people and wounded seven others in the so-called 'Battle of Broken Hill'. The killers were identified as the former cameleers Badsha Mahommed Gool and Mullah Abdullah, who hailed from what is now Afghanistan and Pakistan. They were themselves killed soon after their attacks, but they had left notes indicating that their sympathies lay with the Ottoman Empire, which had joined the war as Germany's ally in October 1914.

Broken Hill had a longstanding German connection. One of the founders of Broken Hill Proprietary Limited was a German, Charles Rasp. Although they had no involvement in the New Year's Day killings, Germans and Austrians became the targets of a local quest for revenge against 'enemy aliens'. One of the first targets was the Broken Hill German Club House. An Australian flag was attached to the flagstaff that remained when the building was destroyed by fire.

That outburst of popular anger was soon matched with official action in the form of the arrest of 'enemy aliens'. Broken Hill was part of the 4th Military District, which had its headquarters in Adelaide, so the dozen men arrested were sent to Adelaide under military escort on 4 January 1915. According to a report in the *Adelaide Chronicle*, the group comprised four Germans, seven Austrians, and a Turk.

The Turk in that group was almost certainly a man by the name of Sulaman Mustala. At least, that is how his name appeared on the official list of internees.

# Theodor Dudic (or Tom Dudich)

Theodor Dudic was one of the Austrians interned on Torrens Island – or at least that is what the authorities thought.

Should Dudic have been interned? At the outbreak of the First World War, Austria-Hungary was a large, multi-ethnic empire which extended into the troubled region of the Balkans. If Dudic was from Austria-Hungary, then he was technically an 'enemy alien'. But if he was from Serbia – which was at war with Austria-Hungary – then there was no case.

Dudic certainly thought himself hard done by when he was interned on Torrens Island on 15 January 1915. He wrote to the Serb consul setting out his grievances. He escaped from Torrens Island on the night of 15 June 1915, but he was recaptured in February 1916 and re-interned, this time in the Holsworthy camp in New South Wales. He continued to make the case that he was Serbian, although the military authorities insisted that he had represented himself to them as an Austrian when he was originally interned.

In April 1916 Dudic was released from custody and remained in Australia after the war, securing his naturalisation in 1921, almost six years to the day after his daring escape.

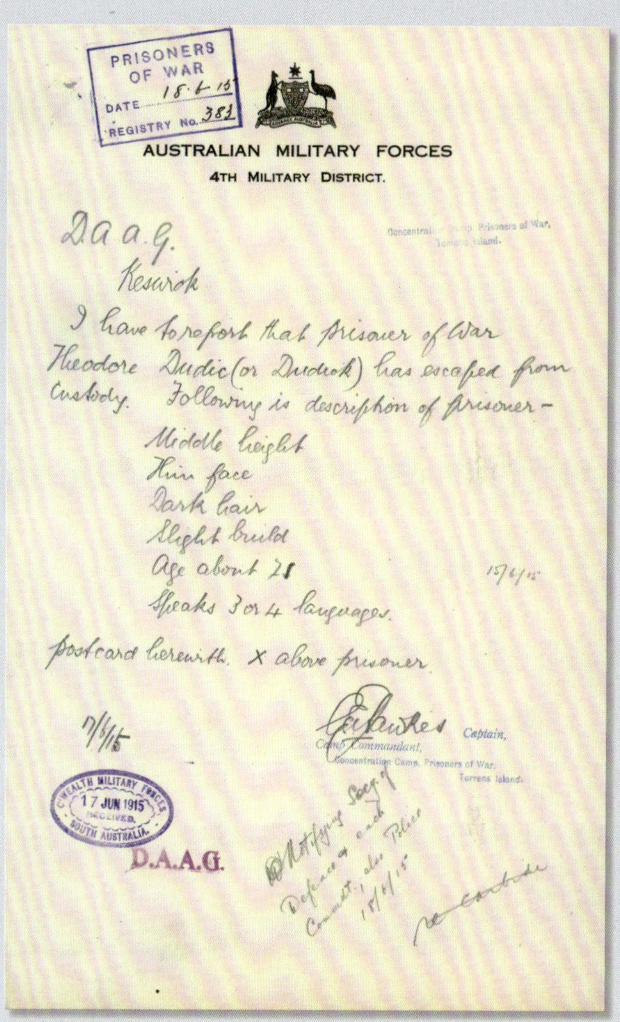

PRISONERS OF WAR
DATE 18.6.15
REGISTRY No. 381

AUSTRALIAN MILITARY FORCES
4TH MILITARY DISTRICT.

Concentration Camp, Prisoners of War, Torrens Island.

D.A.A.G.
Keswick

I have to report that Prisoner of War Theodore Dudic (or Dudock) has escaped from Custody. Following is description of prisoner –

Middle height
Thin face
Dark hair
Slight build
Age about 28
Speaks 3 or 4 languages.

15/6/15

postcard herewith. X above prisoner.

17/6/15

G.E. Hawkes Captain,
Camp Commandant,
Concentration Camp, Prisoners of War,
Torrens Island.

C'WEALTH MILITARY FORCES
17 JUN 1915
RECEIVED.
SOUTH AUSTRALIA.

D.A.A.G.

Notifying Secy of Defence & each Commdt, also Police 18/6/15

In this letter, the Camp Commandant Captain G.E. Hawkes of the 'Concentration Camp, Prisoners of War, Torrens Island' wrote to the Deputy Assistant Adjutant General at Keswick barracks to advise of Dudic's escape.

NAA: D1915, SA444, Dudich, Theodore [or Theodor Duduc or Teodor Dudics] – Melbourne – application for naturalization

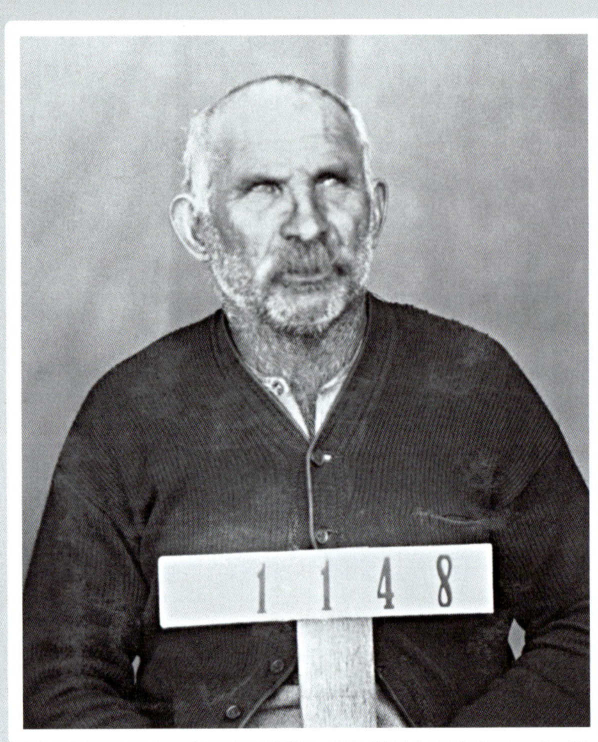


Georg Paul Fischer, photographed for official internment records.

NAA: D3597, 1148, Fischer, Paul

## Georg Paul Fischer

Georg Paul Fischer was interned because he turned down the opportunity of parole. Like many Germans he found it desperately difficult to find employment in Australia after the outbreak of war.

His internment hit his family very hard. His fourteen-year-old daughter Elsie was committed to the state children's department for larceny and placed in a home, then in the Redruth Girls' Reformatory in Burra. Fischer's wife Charlotte was admitted to the Mental Asylum at Parkside in early 1916. An application made by Fischer to visit his ill wife was denied by the military authorities. His stepson became well known to police because of his drinking.

After the war Fischer was released from the camp at Holsworthy and returned to Adelaide in late December 1918. Early the following year he reported to the Keswick Barracks, destitute and unable to find work, so he was re-interned.

# Johann Gerdes

Johann Gerdes arrived in Australia in May 1914. He was among those Germans paroled after the outbreak of war, but on breaking the terms of his parole he was interned on Torrens Island on 8 January 1915.

Later that year he would prove himself a nuisance to military authorities. He escaped from Torrens Island in June 1915 but was recaptured. He claimed to be an American citizen, though had allegedly made no earlier mention of this, nor did he have papers to support his claim.

NAME Johan GERDES
Address 32 Alexander St Collingwood
Nationality German
Place of Birth Sandes
Date of Birth 30/7/86
Single or Married Single
Occupation Weaver (Textile)
Arrived in Australia on 1914.
Port of Adelaide per APENA
Johann Gerdes
SIGNATURE OF HOLDER.
Certificate issued at Melbourne
on 31/5/48
Issued by
For COMMONWEALTH MIGRATION OFFICER.

CANCELLED

DEPARTMENT OF IMMIGRATION 31 MAY 1948 MELBOURNE

1

Personal Description:
Height 5 ft. 6 ins.
Build Slight
Eyes Brown Hair Grey
Remarks Tattoo, Both arms Scar on Shin.

DEPARTMENT OF IMMIGRATION 31 MAY 1948

Johann Gerdes after the Second World War, when he was finally naturalised.

NAA: B78 1955, Gerdes J.

Gerdes was transferred to Holsworthy in August 1915 and then managed to escape again in March of the following year. There is no record that he was recaptured, or at least not during that war. During the Second World War, however, he found himself in Melbourne's Pentridge Prison, having been convicted of assault. Once again he claimed to be an American citizen, and once again he provided no evidence to prove his case. He remained in Australia after the war and was eventually naturalised.

# Max Hemmerdinger

Max Hemmerdinger was born in Heidelberg, Germany, in 1866, and came to South Australia in 1892. When he was naturalised as a British subject in 1903 he was working as a bookbinder and living at Point Pass.

Hemmerdinger was a talented violinist, and the years before and after his naturalisation saw him contribute musical items at many local events in the Point Pass and Eudunda districts. As well as playing his violin, he also recited in German, and was noted in the local press for his 'comic items'. Among the events at which Hemmerdinger performed was a patriotic evening at the Eudunda Unterhaltungs-Club on 24 February 1900, attended by locals from all over this 'Anglo-German district'. The report in the *Register* noted:

> The stage was neatly decorated with the German merchant flag, the Union Jack, and Royal Standard of old England, and other evidences of unity of sentiment, and throughout the long and varied programme . . . the loyalty of the audience was frequently manifested. Mr F.W. Paech, MP, in the capacity of Chairman, presented a graphic picture of the suffering occasioned by the war [in South Africa] now raging, which he asserted could have but one termination, the British victorious.

The next war saw Hemmerdinger, by then a naturalised British subject, interned. He arrived on Torrens Island on 16 June 1915. His stay was a short one, as he was among the two naturalised British subjects granted an unconditional release on 18 August, as the camp was closing. Seven others were among the prisoners transferred to Holsworthy.

## Theodor August Joseph Kleine

One of the most unusual cases of voluntary internment was that of Theodor August Joseph Kleine of Edwardstown, South Australia. Naturalised in Australia in 1911, Kleine made a trip back to Germany in 1914 and was in Berlin when war broke out. As a British subject Kleine was arrested and interned in the Ruhleben camp but was later released and repatriated to Australia. Unable to re-establish himself he was forced to offer himself for internment in May 1916.

Theodor Kleine during his internment at Holsworthy.

NAA: D3597 4282 KLEINE, Theodor

# Alois Hosch

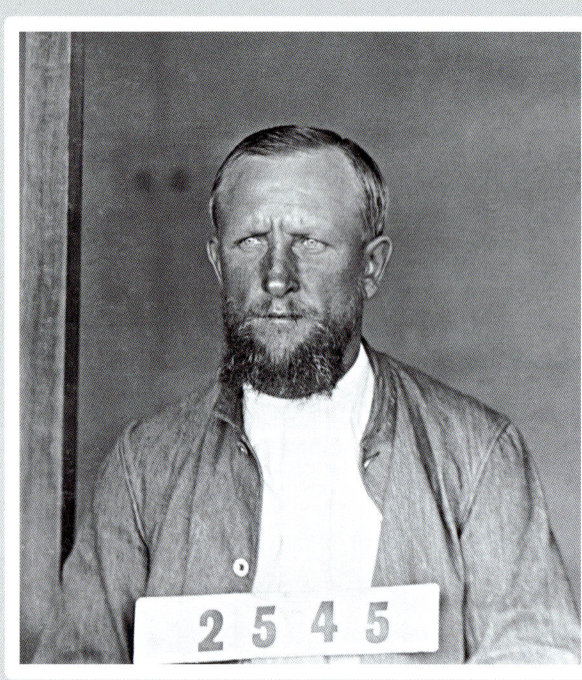


Alois Hosch during his internment at Holsworthy.

NAA: D3597, 2545 HOSCH Alois

Alois Hosch was born in Kosmutz in Germany in 1873. He was interned on Torrens Island from 13 May 1915, and then transferred to the Holsworthy camp at Liverpool in August of that year.

His story is as interesting for what happened outside the camps as for what happened on the inside. The military authorities received encouragement from Hosch's employer to intern him, then his wife and children did what they could to have him released – in vain.

Hosch was deported from Australia on *Tras-os-Montes* in July 1919 but returned to Australia in 1929. He was naturalised in 1936 and yet fell under suspicion once more during the Second World War. After interviewing him in March 1943, Security Service officers described him as a 'sly, cunning, stubborn and truly German in every sense of the word. Truth is an unknown word to him, and being a lover of money he would harm any cause or person if approached in the right way.'

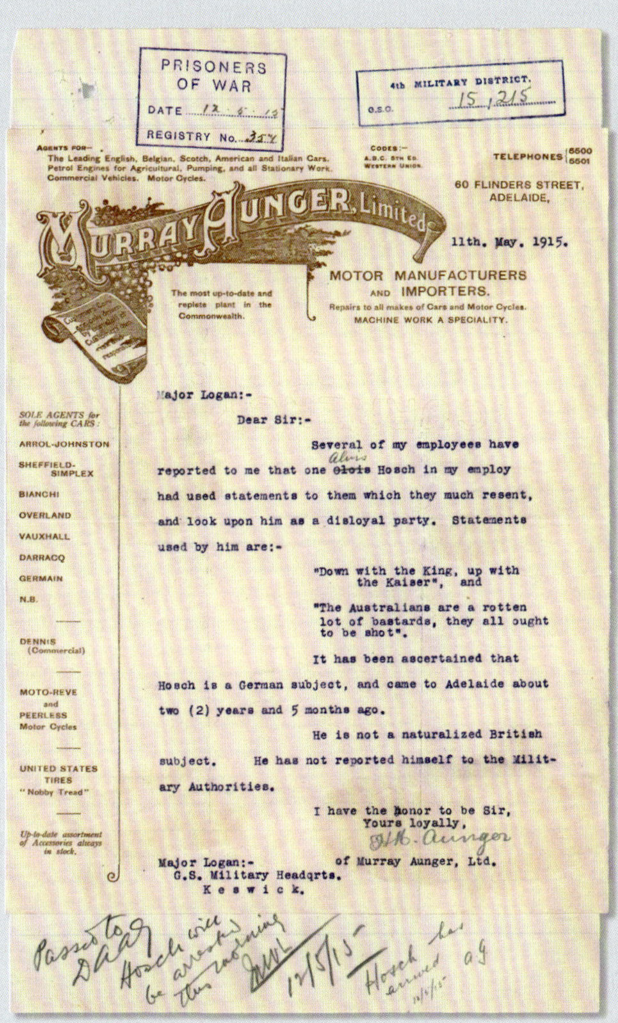

PRISONERS OF WAR
DATE 12.5.15
REGISTRY No. 354

4th MILITARY DISTRICT.
G.S.O. 15/215

AGENTS FOR—
The Leading English, Belgian, Scotch, American and Italian Cars.
Petrol Engines for Agricultural, Pumping, and all Stationary Work.
Commercial Vehicles. Motor Cycles.

CODES:— A.B.C. 5th Ed. Western Union.

TELEPHONES 5500 5501

60 FLINDERS STREET,
ADELAIDE,

MURRAY AUNGER, Limited

The most up-to-date and replete plant in the Commonwealth.

MOTOR MANUFACTURERS AND IMPORTERS.
Repairs to all makes of Cars and Motor Cycles.
MACHINE WORK A SPECIALITY.

SOLE AGENTS for the following CARS: ARROL-JOHNSTON, SHEFFIELD-SIMPLEX, BIANCHI, OVERLAND, VAUXHALL, DARRACQ, GERMAIN, N.B., DENNIS (Commercial), MOTO-REVE and PEERLESS Motor Cycles, UNITED STATES TIRES "Nobby Tread"

Up-to-date assortment of Accessories always in stock.

11th. May. 1915.

Major Logan:-

Dear Sir:-

Several of my employees have reported to me that one ~~Alois~~ Alois Hosch in my employ had used statements to them which they much resent, and look upon him as a disloyal party. Statements used by him are:-

"Down with the King, up with the Kaiser", and

"The Australians are a rotten lot of bastards, they all ought to be shot".

It has been ascertained that Hosch is a German subject, and came to Adelaide about two (2) years and 5 months ago.

He is not a naturalized British subject. He has not reported himself to the Military Authorities.

I have the Honor to be Sir,
Yours loyally,
H. Aunger
of Murray Aunger, Ltd.

Major Logan:-
G.S. Military Headqrts.
K e s w i c k.

Passed to DAAG
Hosch will be arrested this morning
12/5/15
Hosch has arrived

Hosch's employer wrote to the military authorities at Keswick alleging that Hosch was disloyal.

NAA: D1915 SA938, Hosch, Alois

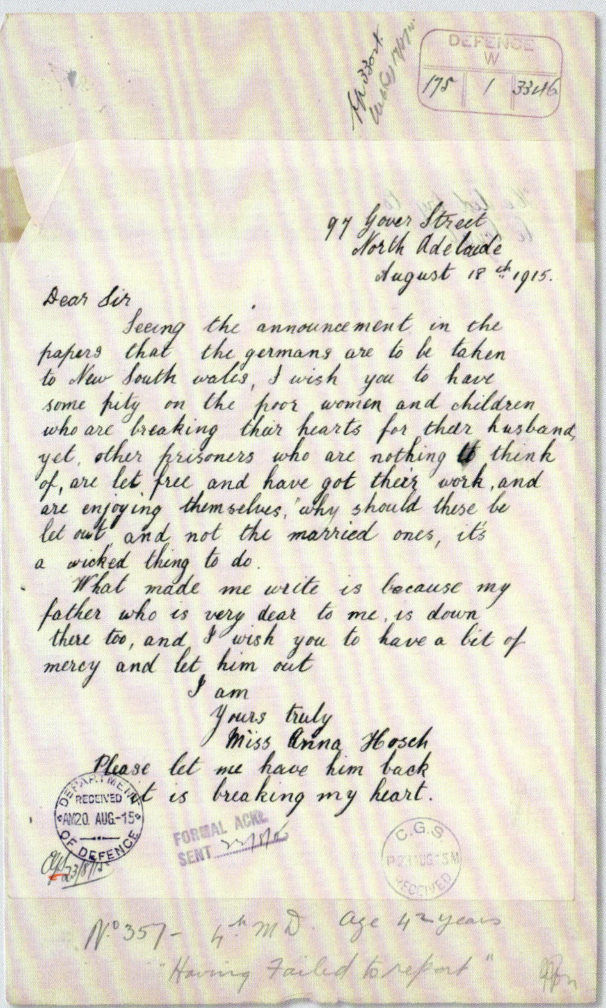

DEFENCE W 175 / 3346

97 Gover Street
North Adelaide
August 18th 1915.

Dear Sir

Seeing the announcement in the papers that the germans are to be taken to New South wales, I wish you to have some pity on the poor women and children who are breaking their hearts for their husband, yet, other prisoners who are nothing to think of, are let free and have got their work, and are enjoying themselves, why should these be let out and not the married ones, it's a wicked thing to do.

What made me write is because my father who is very dear to me, is down there too, and I wish you to have a bit of mercy and let him out

I am
Yours truly
Miss Anna Hosch

Please let me have him back it is breaking my heart.

DEPARTMENT OF DEFENCE RECEIVED AM20 AUG-15

FORMAL ACKN SENT

C.G.S. RECEIVED

No 357 – 4th M.D. Age 42 years
"Having failed to report"

As the internees on Torrens Island were on the brink of their transfer to New South Wales, Hosch's daughter Anna made a heartfelt plea for her father's release.

NAA: D1915 SA938, Hosch, Alois

## Loxton

A disproportionately large number of prisoners came from the Loxton area, where the outbreak of war triggered tensions. There were allegations of a parade of goose-stepping Germans down the main street of Loxton on 25 October 1914. One of their ringleaders was said to be a German-born butcher by the name of Karl Wilhelm Lude. Further accusations had it that a couple of days later Lude pulled a weapon on the local policeman Richard Alfred Lenthall and threatened to kill him.

Accusations of disloyalty among Germans in the Loxton area persisted through the war. At various points it was alleged that very few of them volunteered for service in the AIF, that many carried firearms in defiance of regulations concerning 'enemy aliens', and that a group of them had toasted the sinking of the *Lusitania*.

After the war a commission was conducted to investigate these claims. According to its report, altogether 103 men from the Loxton district were interned during the war, close to 10 per cent of the German population. This compares with just 33 internees from Tanunda, who made up only 3.15 per cent of the German population there.

The arrest and detention of 'enemy aliens' required the cooperation of police and military authorities. Here Loxton Mounted Constables Lenthall and Smith, accompanied by three military figures, gather Han Frohlick, Fritz Wilhelm Lessemann, Phillip Glassen and Johann August Schulz for transport to Adelaide on 10 October 1914. Lenthall seems to have been particularly enthusiastic in the performance of such duties, with the result that a disproportionately large number of Germans were interned from the Loxton district.

Courtesy South Australian Police Historical Society Inc

## Anton Peter Matulovich

When Anton Peter Matulovich was born in 1883, his Dalmatian homeland was part of Austria-Hungary. He arrived in Australia in 1912 and was working in the South Mine at Broken Hill at the time the war broke out. He was one of the 'enemy aliens' interned on 6 January 1915 in response to the 'Broken Hill Massacre'.

Matulovich must have been released on parole from Torrens Island and returned to Broken Hill, because records show that he enlisted in the Australian Imperial Force, the AIF, in October 1916. Then it was discovered that he was an 'enemy alien' who had passed himself off as a Russian. He was arrested and placed back in internment in October 1916, first in Fort Largs, then in Holsworthy. After the war he was repatriated. By that time the place of his birth was no longer Austria-Hungary but the newly created state of Yugoslavia.

Anton Matulovich in internment.

NAA: D3597, 3832, Matulovich, Toni

## Martin Trojan

Martin Trojan was interned on Torrens Island in May 1915. In a book written after the war he described his trip to Torrens Island like this:

> The last night in Port Pirie, where I had lived for two-and-a-half years. I had a very heavy heart. 'It is God's wish that I must be separated from that which I hold most dear. Farewell, Gwen! If it is God's wish, good-bye!'
>
> 3 May 1915. We rose very early and prepared to travel. A large crowd received fifty of us at the railway station. The transport leader refused us permission to smoke, because we were singing 'Die Wacht am Rhein' ['The Watch on the Rhine', a German patriotic anthem] when the train started moving. In Adelaide we changed trains for Port Adelaide. As I could only walk slowly because of my heavy luggage, Sergeant M. jabbed me in my side with his rifle butt. The whole day long we were able to feed our empty stomachs with just one bread roll.
>
> In the cold, pitch-black night we had to walk from the Port Adelaide station to the harbour. Singing we climbed aboard a little boat, and we sang as we travelled across the water to 'Torrens Island', the devil's island. We disembarked and were once more subjected to a close inspection. Everyone received a blanket, and then we went into the camp.
>
> On 'Torrens' we found 314 Germans and Austrians already there; some sympathetic souls among them gave us something to eat. This was now the third night on which I had not been able to change my clothes. In a state of exhaustion I sank down into my place on the sandy ground, thought of my Gwen and of other dear friends, until sleep pulled me from my heavy lamentations and embraced me in its charitable arms.
>
> 4 May 1915. The first little stories, which the people already in the camp had to tell, were of a truly gruesome nature. They were of bayonet jabs, with the not exactly comforting addition that this activity was becoming more common among the soldiers here; a shiver ran down my spine. During the night a shot had been fired, but we could not find out why. I learned that to date three prisoners had attempted to escape, and one of them had drowned in the process. Because of the danger of sharks it is extremely difficult and daring to make a successful escape and brave the waters.
>
> [. . .]
>
> Oh, how barren it is here! No houses, no flowers. Sand, sand and a miserable bit of bush.

Martin Trojan after his transfer to Holsworthy camp in 1915.

NAA: D3597, 4750, TROJAN, Martin

# The War Precautions Act

The primary purpose of the Commonwealth *War Precautions Act 1914* was to ensure the security of Australia and its allies during the war. During the second reading speech, Senator George Pearce, the Minister for Defence, outlined its object as follows: 'It is designed entirely to meet conditions inseparable from the war, to provide for effective measures being adopted for the safety of Australia and for taking due steps to see that no assistance of any kind can be rendered to the enemies of the Empire'. The Act provided statutory authority for actions taken by the executive, and enabled orders and regulations to be swiftly enacted in order to serve the defence of the Commonwealth.

The Act was rushed through under suspended standing orders, and those who may have wished to oppose or amend it had little opportunity to do so. As William Higgs noted in the House of Representatives, 'I do not rise to oppose the Bill, because it was introduced only an hour ago, and I have, therefore, not had an opportunity to properly study it.'

In addition to being used to authorise the system of internment, which had already begun prior to its enactment, the Act was also used to prevent trading with the enemy and, later, to prevent the proliferation of anti-conscription propaganda. Sections 4 and 5 of the Act, which provided the Governor-General with the authority to make certain provisions and regulations, were integral to providing statutory authority for the internment system. The wide powers granted to the Governor-General were the subject of some criticism. Attorney-General Billy Hughes defended those powers:

> It is the wish of the Government not to take any more powers than are absolutely necessary to meet the case. The preservation of the safety of the Commonwealth is not a milk-and-water business. We cannot fit the purpose with a Bill giving the requisite powers and then deal with offenders with feather dusters. That we have to deal with possible enemies and people who are clever and cunning must be recognised, and that the machinery to deal with them should be in the possession of civilization and organized society. The Government seek for nothing more than is necessary to meet situations of emergency and difficulty.

Essentially it was a matter of trusting the government to use the powers appropriately. The Act was proclaimed on 29 October 1914.

The powers of the Act and the implementation of regulations authorised by the Act were the subject of the landmark High Court *Lloyd v. Wallach* case. This case challenged an application of regulation 55, which allowed for the Minister for Defence to issue warrants for the detention in military custody of naturalised persons he had reason to believe were 'disaffected or disloyal'. The High Court ruled that the minister merely needed to have 'reason to believe' a person was disloyal in order to detain him or her. As the minister could claim privilege against disclosing the rationale for this belief, these warrants could be rendered non-appealable. The case is significant as it is an example of the suspension of the principle of *Habeas corpus*; the nature of the war and the *War Precautions Act* allowed for actions to be conducted and rights to be suspended that would not have been sanctioned in peacetime.

The Act was repealed by the *War Precautions Repeal Act* on 2 December 1920.

This panorama by Paul Dubotzki shows the camp at its second location, at the southern tip of Torrens Island. The main compound with its orderly rows of tents is bordered on two sides by the makeshift 'kitchens' constructed by the prisoners out of sticks, hessian sacks and corrugated iron.

State Library of South Australia, B 12161

# 4. Torrens Island Concentration Camp

Torrens Island is a low-lying island in the Port River estuary, isolated by its geography but within easy reach of Port Adelaide. Long and narrow, the island runs north-south, bordered with narrow beaches and mangroves. It had been the location of a quarantine station since the mid-1850s, and in October 1914 it became the site of Torrens Island internment camp. Initially located adjacent to the quarantine station on the north of the island, the camp was moved in early 1915 to the southern part of the island.

Life inside the camp was documented by two internees, photographer Paul Dubotzki and diarist Frank Bungardy, a boxer who was working in the mines at Broken Hill when he was arrested and interned. It also generated official records – notably, the evidence given in a series of enquiries into events on the island. While these accounts do not always agree, there is enough common ground to be able to draw a general outline of camp life.

Prisoners travelled by train to Port Adelaide, were taken under guard from the station to the wharves, and then by boat to the island. As Bungardy put it: 'Ones the gate closed behind us, we wher inside of the barbwire fence, our future home'.[1]

Prisoners and guards alike referred to the main compound as 'the German lines'. This area housed most of those interned.[2] Officers, including August Strycker, former captain of SS *Scharzfels*, were held in a separate part of the camp. Guards also lived on site, occupying available buildings or living under canvas.

## 'The German lines'

In the main compound, seven or eight prisoners were allocated to each tent. Each prisoner was issued a waterproof sheet, two blankets and the makings of a mattress. Bungardy, who recorded that he was not issued with any straw to stuff his 'sack' and form a mattress, described how the men in his crowded tent 'layd hudled together like Pigs in a stye during the nights'.[3]

## Paul Dubotzki

Paul Dubotzki was born in Ingolstadt, Germany, in 1891 and spent many of the early years of his life in Passau. As a young man he learned the craft of photography, and in that capacity joined a German expedition to Southeast Asia in 1913. At the outbreak of war he was in New Guinea, where he witnessed the mobilisation of German forces.

It is not clear how Dubotzki ended up in Adelaide in the second half of 1914, but he was recorded as living at 232 Rundle Street, presumably on parole. Records show that he was interned on Torrens Island by 1 February 1915.

In a move they might have come to regret, the military authorities allowed him to keep his camera, which he used to make an invaluable photographic record of life in the Torrens Island camp. He did the same when he was later transferred to the camps at Liverpool (Holsworthy) and Trial Bay in New South Wales. But it was on Torrens Island that he received his first taste of Australian military discipline and of life in a 'concentration camp'.

After the war Dubotzki was repatriated aboard *Kursk* in May 1919 and settled in the Bavarian town of Dorfen, just outside Munich, where he re-established his career as a photographer. He died in 1969, though happily the images he made in internment in Australia survive.

On the other side of the camera: Paul Dubotzki as an internee.

NAA: 3597 4838, Dubotzki, Paul

## Frank Bungardy

Among the dozen men sent under military escort to Adelaide after the 'Broken Hill Massacre' was Frank Bungardy. Married with two young children, Bungardy's brother-in-law, Arthur Klopp, had joined the AIF and would soon be serving at Gallipoli. None of that, however, saved Bungardy from internment.

On his official prisoner of war card Bungardy is identified as a 'pugilist', a boxer. The description tallies well with the picture of him, showing his flattened boxer nose and his cauliflower ears. In numerous bouts fought in rural Australia he acquired the nicknames the 'Bun' and 'The Iron-Jawed German'. On the eve of war he was an employee in a mine in Broken Hill.

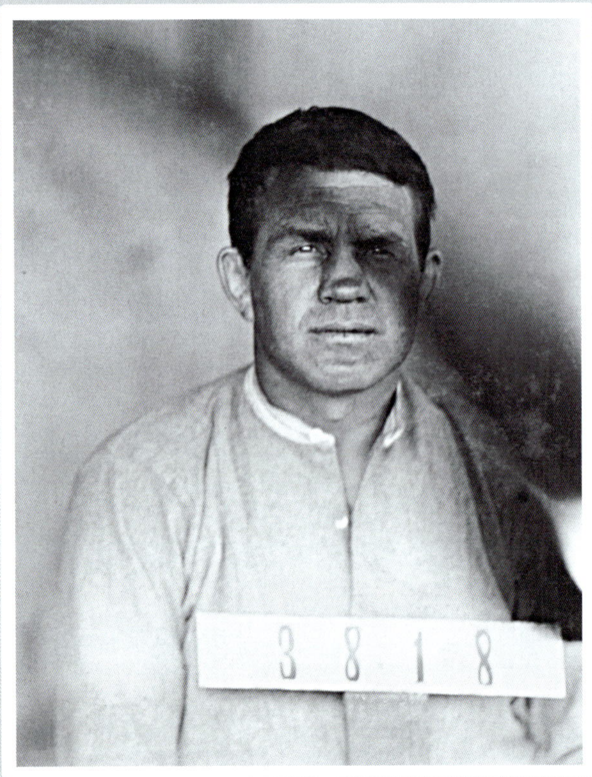


Frank Bungardy after his transfer to the camp at Holsworthy.

NAA: D3597 3818, Bungardy, Frank

Bungardy later described his arrest in the following way:

> I wher called upon by a Constable and ordered to the Police Station under arrest. On our arrival I wher informed, to consider myself in custody as a Prisoner of War. The reason for my arrest as stated wher 'failing to report'. This acusation wher a false one as I had reported myself weekly, my last report being 3 days previous to my arrest. The News to consider myself under arrest of course wher a great shock at first, especially as I had a Wife and Children at home, awaiting Fathers return from work. I wher permitted to goe home to get some personal effects. The time granted being half an hour. Owing the short time allowance, my 'good by' to the dear ones I wher forced to leave behind, wher a short one. Heavy hearthed in charge of a Detective, I left my home, a weeping wife, and my weeping children, bound for the Railway station, to catch the Adelaide Express.

Just a few days before Bungardy was transferred from Torrens Island to the Holsworthy camp at Liverpool in New South Wales, on 10 August 1915, Arthur Klopp was killed in action at Gallipoli.

During his transfer from South Australia Bungardy made his escape by jumping from the train. He was recaptured and served out the rest of the war – and beyond – in Holsworthy. He was repatriated on *Valencia* in October 1919, without his wife and two children, who remained in Adelaide. Not long after his return to Germany Bungardy died as a result of a knockout blow received during a bout in Kiel.

Days were punctuated by roll call and the distribution of rations at three o'clock each afternoon. Rations were distributed by tent, and consisted of meat, potatoes, coffee, sugar, bread, jam, salt, pepper, and some vegetables. Those who had the funds could order extra stores through the quartermaster, as well as tobacco and clothes. Prisoners were also issued a cooking pot, tin plate, tin mug, fork, spoon and knife. They used kerosene tins purchased from the quartermaster to fashion other items – Bungardy mentions a coffee kettle, frying pan, water bucket 'and various other cooking utensils'.[4]

The men in Bungardy's tent took the role of cook by turns, for a week at a time. They rigged up both a 'kitchen' and 'dining room':

> Owing our tent being small, and very inconvenient to use it as Bedroom, Kitchen and Dinning Room combined, we wher forced to procure bags at 4p a piece, old Potatoe Bags. Went out into the Bushe under guard, procured some sticks, and we soon had a rough and ready Bush Kitchen and dining room. Our Kitchen contained a fireplace, made out of a few stones and mudd, to which a few Iron Bars wher addet, for the Pots to stand on, a rough bench for the Pots to stand on when not in use. The Dining Room contained two rough Benches, around a ditto table, with a Butter-box in one corner as a safe. Our cooler, owing the hot season, being another box wich we procured through the officer in charge for wich we paid, sunk into the ground.

The sandy conditions made cooking difficult. Bungardy complained that 'the Cook only had to lift the lid of the cooking pot, when a hand full of sand wher laying on top of the stew, instead of the necessary pepper'.[5]

Sanitary provisions at the camp were rudimentary. The prisoners dug pits in the sand into which they emptied waste water. Urinals and latrines were also pits, screened on one side with corrugated iron sheet. Prisoners covered old pits and dug new ones each day. Soap for washing, including clothes, was issued every three weeks. Bungardy noted wryly that those who could not afford extra soap were prey to vermin, 'in fact the quantity wher almost equall of Germanys fighting force'.[6]

## Marking time

Those men who were not occupied doing tasks around the camp such as collecting wood, digging latrines and cooking, had empty days to fill in bleak surroundings.

Prisoners were not allowed books or newspapers. Correspondence was permitted, and prisoners could send two letters each week. Letters in and out of the camp were censored, an exception to the general rule that the Commonwealth censor was not concerned with mail within Australia. Bungardy wrote that 'anything written, stating of our ill treatment, or us asking for money, never wher passed, but went into the wastepaper basket'. Prisoners were required to pay for postage, which rankled, as they were aware that this contravened the Hague Convention. Prisoners were also permitted short visits from their families. The visits took place on the jetty, under guard, and lasted only as long as it took to unload from the motor launch whatever it was delivering to the camp.[7]

Those interned on Torrens Island found ways to relieve the monotony. Bungardy wrote of gambling, cards and two-up being played from 'morning until late at nights', until a notice was issued banning gambling of any sort. After this, two-up ceased, but card-playing continued – including poker. Bungardy noted that although raids and arrests of tentfuls of men for gambling were frequent, the prisoners were permitted to purchase as many packs of cards as they could afford.[8]

In June 1915 the prisoners produced three issues of a handwritten and illustrated newspaper. *Der Kamerad* included advertisements for businesses within the camp, including Electra tattoos and the Kaiser Café. Paul Dubotzki's photographic studio offered portraits as well as photographs of the camp in cabinet or postcard format.[9]

Music provided amusement and consolation. Prisoners organised a choir and more than one band. Bungardy wrote of a sailors' band, with two accordions, several mouth organs, and improvised triangle, kettle drum and big drum. He also observed:

> . . . later on we had also a Brass Band. Many a long weary hour during the hot evenings we amused ourself, laying in a circle in the soft sand enjoying German Ballats, dittis, Soldiers and National songs. If it hadnt been for this their would have been a few more driven mad.[10]

## Celebrating the Kaiser's birthday

Kaiser Wilhelm II's birthday, 27 January 1915, provided a distraction and outlet for ingenuity for weeks. Prisoners who were German reservists drilled for the parade march. Bungardy wrote of the uniforms:

> The rifles used wher made out of sticks and broom handles. Every Soldiers wher dressed alike. Blue trousers, white shirt, white cap. The caps were made out of white handkerchiefs.

That only left the problem of how to outfit the prisoners who would play the emperor, the high officials, and the ladies.

# Der Kamerad

A number of prisoners worked together to produce three hand-drawn issues of a camp newspaper they titled *Der Kamerad*, which translates to *The Comrade*, subtitled 'Weekly paper of the prisoners of war, Torrens Island, South Australia'. Edited by Walter Emde, it contained literary works, artwork, and even some advertising for the small businesses that some of the prisoners established in the camp. One of the businesses that advertised was the studio of photographer Paul Dubotzki; the address provided was 'Hauptstrasse 5, Torrens Island' (5 Main Street, Torrens Island). Another was for a tattoo parlour, while still another was for the Kaiser Café.

The newspaper provided an outlet for some considerable talents and for some humour. In the second issue, for example, one of the internees announced that he was opening a flying school; another offered to build ships and submarines.

All three issues were published in June 1915, a period when relations between prisoners and the commandant were very strained. With tight military censorship, there was a limit to what could be published. When the third issue was in preparation, the editors already knew it would be the last. They published in it an 'open letter' to Major Logan at Keswick Barracks complaining of the maltreatment of prisoners in the camp.

DER KAMERAD

WOCHENSCHRIFT der KRIEGSGEFANGENEN aus TORRENS ISLAND SÜD AUSTRALIEN

HERAUSGEBER: W. EMDE.

19 JUNI 1915

The front page of *Der Kamerad*, No. 2, 19 June 1915.

Courtesy State Library of South Australia

> We made the spiked Helmets out of kerosine tins, soldered together. Swallow tail coats and evening frocks cut off at the bottom part, with yellow painted buttones, suitable brocade and tin medals galore, substituted, the smart Officers jacket. White trousers made into Riding breeches, seaboots and spurs, borrowed from some civil interned boundary Riders, completed the Uniform.

Six prisoners were transformed into 'nice and handsome' ladies with dresses cut by an internee who was an 'expert cutter' from material purchased through the stores and hats made from fencing wire, cloth and paper flowers. The final touch was long hair, made out of dyed rope.[11]

On the evening of 26 January, the German band led a procession 'according to German custom', through the camp, carrying torches fashioned out of broken bottles and candles. After breakfast the following morning was the parade. Then followed sporting competitions, with cash prizes, and, that night, singing and dancing. Bungardy recalled:

> We fancied ourself holding a curtlady in our arms and walzing around the emperors palace untill the haevy sandy ground remindet us, that we wher on Australian soil, the handsome lady, a fellow sufferer like ourself.[12]

## Under guard

The prisoners shared the island with their guards. Drawn largely from the 23rd Light Horse Regiment and the 78th Infantry Battalion, they were among those who served in home defence duties during the war.

Since 1911 all fit, eligible males between the ages of 18 and 26 had been required to serve in the Citizen Military Forces, also known as the militia. That meant that when war broke out in 1914, large numbers of young South Australian men had received some military training. The *Defence Act* limited overseas service to volunteers, and many of those in the militia volunteered for service in the Australian Imperial Force, the AIF. Others served at home, in a range of duties such as providing guards for internment camps including Torrens Island.

There was no shortage of guards on Torrens Island, indeed at times the guards seem to have nearly outnumbered the prisoners. Bungardy recognised that the boredom of life on the island was a problem shared by prisoners and guards alike, and that the two groups of men lived in similar physical conditions.

Before the appointment of Captain George Edward Hawkes as camp commandant in early 1915, relations between guards and prisoners were familiar and discipline quite relaxed. When Hawkes's predecessor Captain Butler was transferred to other work within the District Headquarters, Hawkes was appointed in his place owing to his reputation as a firm disciplinarian. He took up his post at about the time that the camp was moved from its position adjacent to the quarantine station to the southern end of the island.[13] The change of tone in the camp during Hawkes's tenure might never have become known outside the camp, except that word got out of abuses being perpetrated on prisoners by Hawkes and his men. As a result, the military authorities had to confront some awkward truths.

It was the prisoners themselves who managed to raise the alarm. On the night of 19 June 1915, two prisoners, Johann Gerdes and Wilhelm Holmann, escaped from Torrens Island. They got out through the drains, took a boat and crossed the Port River. They were recaptured in the Adelaide Hills and returned to Torrens Island on 24 June. According to their own accounts, they were then handcuffed together, ordered to stop at a tree, and told by a Sergeant Mackintosh that they were going to be shot. They had their hands tied to the tree, with their shirts pulled over their heads and their trousers pulled down. They were reportedly given thirty strokes with the cat-o'-nine-tails and then taken to the camp hospital, where some salve was applied to their wounds.[14]

These events might have had no further consequences, except that there was photographic evidence of them provided by Paul Dubotzki and his camera. How that came about was recalled in an interview many years later by one of the former guards, Harold Tilley, who was in the camp at the time of the floggings:

> Anyhow, they thrashed them that bad that they had to put them in the hospital tent, you see. So Paul Grabowski [Dubotzki], he was a photographer . . . asked where they were and how he could get into the hospital tent to take a photo. [Dubotzki] took a photo, and it was smuggled in a boot taken for repair in town, was sent to State Commandant Colonel Sanders [Augustus Henry Sandford].[15]

In case that effort to draw attention to their plight did not work, the prisoners also tried another avenue. In the third – and final – issue of their camp newspaper *Der Kamerad*, they wrote an open letter of appeal to the military authorities at Keswick.

## George Edward Hawkes

Detail of a group photo by Paul Dubotzki showing Hawkes. Dubotzki wrote on the reverse of the photo 'In the middle of the image is the bastard [*Schweinehund*] of a commandant who at the most minor offence had us Germans lashed with his whip on our naked flesh or worked over with the bayonet.'

State Library of South Australia, B46796 [detail]

From early 1915 the commanding officer at Torrens Island was George Edward Hawkes, a thirty-seven-year-old bank teller from Glenelg. Hawkes's military service had begun in 1901 as a member of the Glenelg Defence Rifle Club. In 1904 he joined the 10th Australian Infantry Regiment (the Adelaide Rifles, later renamed the 78th Battalion) which had been formed the previous year from the active volunteer battalions, and he was commissioned as an officer in the Citizen Military Force (CMF). In 1908 Hawkes passed the prescribed examination for promotion to captain.

In the year the war began Hawkes was a member of the Headquarters Staff at the new Keswick Barracks – at that time known as the Unley Barracks – serving under Brigadier-General Irving, the Commandant of the 4th Military District. By the following year Hawkes was recorded as commanding officer of the 77th Infantry Battalion, raised in 1915 as a CMF battalion. Unlike the Australian Imperial Force (AIF), which was raised explicitly for overseas service, the soldiers of the CMF served only on Australian soil.

After it was established that Hawkes had presided over the abuse of prisoners on Torrens Island, his commission was cancelled. Hawkes joined the AIF in February 1918 and was sent to Europe. He experienced the last weeks of the war in Europe as a member of the 8th Field Ambulance.

It read:

> Two prisoners of war have been whipped, naked and in public, as a punishment for escaping. We find this punishment unjustified and beneath our dignity. We appeal to the sense of justice of the Major and ask for an investigation.

It was signed 'The Prisoners of War'.[16]

## The first court of enquiry

Exactly how Colonel Sandford, the recently appointed military commandant in South Australia, learned of the allegations of abuse is not clear, but he did make the trip from Keswick to Torrens Island in July, and he made some enquiries. The captain of *Scharzfels*, August Strycker, gave Sandford credible evidence that two prisoners had indeed been flogged. Sandford saw himself obliged to stage an enquiry, and he suspended Captain Hawkes pending the enquiry's findings.[17]

The court of enquiry, presided over by Colonel James Hewell, was held on Torrens Island on 10 August 1915; its other members were Major J.J. Hughes and Captain C.B. Butler. It was quite an informal affair. Besides Johann Gerdes and Wilhelm Holmann providing their accounts of the events, Paul Dubotzki was questioned over his photographs. Captain Hawkes provided his perspective, as did Sidney Campbell Marshall, a guard who did not witness the whipping, but who gave evidence of the insolence of the prisoners. The camp's quartermaster William Arnold Purvis, who did observe the whippings, also acted as a witness for Captain Hawkes.[18]

With Dubotzki's photographic evidence at hand, the fact of the whippings could hardly be disputed. Hawkes and his witnesses took the line that the actions had been justified as a response to the alleged ongoing hostility and insolence displayed by the prisoners. Moreover, Hawkes argued that prisoners had threatened further escapes, because the punishment in the case of being caught 'was nothing to be frightened of'. The court was sympathetic to this argument, noting that the whippings were a reaction to insolence and insubordination, and that they had brought about a marked improvement in the behaviour of the prisoners.[19]

Higher authorities were not quite so tolerant of Hawkes's disciplinary regime. After the enquiry the matter was passed on to the adjutant general of the 4th Military District, who in consulting the *Military Manual* – the official body of regulations which laid down standards of proper military conduct – determined that the commandant could not go unpunished. Hawkes's commission was cancelled – he was dismissed from the Army and lost his rank. In justifying his decision, the adjutant general noted, 'the flogging of prisoners can only have the effect of bringing the Empire into disrepute and probably would lead, if it became known in enemy countries, to reprisals against our own men who are held as prisoners'.[20]

The enquiry was an entirely internal affair; in a time of tight censorship, there were no headlines in the local press to let the people of Adelaide know what was happening on their doorstep. It was quite possible that events on Torrens Island would not become widely known. Moreover, as the camp was in the process of being shut down at that time, the cancellation of its commandant's commission might easily have passed unnoticed.

However, news about other abuses on Hawkes's watch had already been leaking out of the camp, even before Holmann and Gerdes were flogged. As early as 17 April 1915 one of the prisoners, Walter Emde, a German sailor taken from *Kilmallie*, had written to the American consul general – at this time the United States was a neutral power – outlining several complaints. This letter was sent to be translated prior to reaching the consul general, and then it remained with the censor for almost four months before it was returned, translated, to the district military headquarters in Adelaide, by which time the first enquiry had already taken place.[21]

This time the matter went as far as the desk of Minister for Defence George Pearce. When Pearce finally received the translated letter – in early 1916 – a second enquiry was ordered. The American interest in allegations of abuses on Torrens Island was reinforced when the consul general received another letter of complaint, this time from Johann Gerdes, whose flogging had led to the first enquiry, and who now claimed to possess American citizenship. And if that were not troubling enough, it became evident that the allegations had reached as far as Berlin, with the result that the German Foreign Office encouraged inspections of Australian camps to gather more evidence about the treatment of prisoners – evidence which could be presented at the second enquiry.[22]

## The second court of enquiry

The second enquiry took place between April and June 1916 at the Holsworthy camp – by then the home of most of the prisoners from Torrens Island – and in

Adelaide. It was presided over by Major Walter Leslie Stuart, and it called a total of sixty witnesses, among them thirty-five prisoners and fifteen guards.[23]

This was a much more substantial enquiry than the first, and, as earlier, there were multiple claims and counter-claims. Nonetheless, for all the differences of views and recollections, it was apparent that the behaviour of Hawkes and his men had earned the ire and lasting resentment of their prisoners.

There was no need for this second enquiry to revisit the flogging of Holmann and Gerdes – that had been dealt with at the first enquiry, and Hawkes had paid a price. There was, however, a litany of other allegations to be aired at the second enquiry. In the broader scheme of things, some of them were relatively minor, yet symptomatic of the poisoned atmosphere Hawkes had introduced to the camp. Insulting language, probably traded both ways, became part of everyday life on the island. 'German bastards' was a common form of address, deeply resented by the prisoners. The camp interpreter Ernst Baumann recounted a guard removing the German flag from Baumann's cap by throwing it forcefully to the ground, spitting on it and saying 'so much for your fucking flag you bastard'. Perhaps the most colourful language of all was reported by the prisoner Heinrich von Zülow. Once on the way to the latrines a guard warned him, 'if you go crawling about like this I will put a blue bullet into you that will make you shit elephants and spew machine guns, you bloody bastard'.[24]

That kind of crude invective, however, paled into insignificance next to other allegations. Some of these stemmed from a particular event, the so-called 'shed incident'. It was alleged by the prisoners – but denied by Hawkes – that on a particular morning one or two men had been granted permission to scavenge wood and iron from a disused shed in order to improve their makeshift kitchen shelters. A large number of prisoners then proceeded to dismantle the structure, provoking the intervention of the guards. In the testimony of those guards, what followed amounted to a riot, which was brought to a conclusion by detaining a considerable number of prisoners in the camp's punishment cell. It was at this point that an open-air detention compound was constructed of barbed wire between poles measuring about three by five or six metres.[25] Moved from the tiny cell to the detention compound, the arrested men were told to hand over their coats and were kept there overnight, in the rain.

This incident led to six prisoners identified by Lieutenant Parkes and Major John Hardie as ringleaders being sent to Adelaide Gaol for three weeks for demolishing government property. They were Otto Brechlin, Fred Müller, Heinrich Prengl, Ralph Schmidt, August Haucke and Gustav Lange. Those remaining were kept in the open detention compound for between two and three weeks.[26]

Whether the men should have been punished at all was itself a matter of some dispute. It was especially questionable in the case of an elderly prisoner by the name of Georg Fischer, who was among those kept in the compound for two weeks. Fischer at the time was reportedly suffering poor health and was unlikely to have committed the acts for which he was punished.[27]

Then there were allegations of an even more serious nature. The gravest was that Hawkes and his men had been involved in the shooting of prisoners. At the enquiry it became evident that these allegations had more than a little substance. Above all, Hawkes admitted to shooting one particular prisoner, Arthur Rätzsch, in the leg. This occurred on the day after the 'shed incident'. Once again it was Captain Strycker of *Scharzfels* who gave compelling evidence. Cross-examined by Hawkes, Strycker baldly stated, 'I saw you take out your revolver, and I saw you shoot into the compound. I saw two or three shots fired and the next moment I heard one of the men cry out. Later on I saw him coming out of his tent, then I saw him taken away to the hospital.' Hawkes's self-exculpatory explanation, on the other hand, had it that he fired three shots in an attempt to quell a restive group near Rätzsch's tent, then heard a request for cigarette and the word 'monkey'. He fired the fourth shot at Rätzsch, as he believed him responsible for the remarks and insults.[28]

Whatever the provocation, there was no doubt the commandant had shot a prisoner, and there was evidence that others, too, had resorted to firing shots to assert control. One prisoner, Fritz Schröder, testified that guards had been ordered to fire upon prisoners attempting escape and on those who used offensive language regarding the guards or the royal family. Hawkes himself conceded that there had been almost daily shootings in the camp, but he sought to persuade the court that many of these were targeted at rabbits.[29]

Similarly grave were the allegations of the guards' use of bayonets, and multiple prisoners testified to this practice. Here, too, the photographic evidence provided by Paul Dubotzki told a tale that was difficult to deny. The bayonet wounds sustained by the prisoner Wilhelm Matzelt, like Johann Gerdes' flogging wounds, were captured in photographs and tendered as evidence. Matzelt was allegedly bayoneted when, on leaving his tent, he ran into some guards. They told him to 'go on' and then proceeded to bayonet him three times, before allowing him to respond.[30]

Other allegations concerned the brutal treatment of prisoners suffering mental health problems. Bernhardt Wandert reported that Mecke Beyer, who was 'not quite sane', was bayonetted by two guards and then brought to the small compound and handcuffed. Georg Fischer recounted the experience of the 'lunatic man' Frank (or Franz) Rechtenwald, whom Fischer allegedly saw with a battered head while under escort; fourteen days later Rechtenwald cut his own throat. Fortunately he survived this trauma and other abuses and was eventually transferred to the Parkside Lunatic Asylum.[31]

Those who spoke in defence of Hawkes at the second enquiry generally followed the line of defence which had been well received at the first. The claims against Hawkes, these witnesses contended, were distorted or exaggerated; in any case the actions taken in the camp by Hawkes and his men had served the greater good of preserving order in the camp.

It was a line of argument to which the second court, like the first, was receptive, as evident from its findings. The use of bayonets, the court concluded, was justified as a last resort. Confronted with photographic evidence, the court also concluded that the bayonet wounds inflicted on all but Matzelt were slight, and even that Matzelt's wounds were exaggerated in the photograph. Shooting a prisoner, on the other hand, was no slight matter. The court asserted that the only justification of it was 'in cases of attempted escapes, or organised revolt'. As it was found that these conditions were not present at the time of the shooting of Rätzsch, the officer's conduct was judged as hasty and unjustifiable.[32]

Some credibility was conceded to the prisoners on one important issue, and that was the 'shed incident'. Fischer was found to have been incapable of contributing to the shed's destruction, as he was over sixty years of age and suffering from blood poisoning in both hands. The court acknowledged that the failure to have a proper investigation made into the incident at the time resulted in innocent people, including Fischer, being imprisoned. However, the enquiry president also found that the compound in which prisoners were held as punishment was not overly full, and that prisoners had intentionally pushed into a part of the enclosure while the photograph was being taken to give the impression of overcrowding. It was further found that no harm was caused to prisoners as a result of their confinement in the compound; indeed it had been necessary to segregate unruly prisoners from the rest of the camp.[33]

The enquiry revealed Hawkes's direct role in a number of abuses, and as commandant he had to be held accountable for abuses committed by others. Despite the new revelations that emerged from the second enquiry the military authorities decided not to punish Hawkes further and felt that the earlier cancellation of his commission amounted to sufficient punishment. The second court did, however, note that Hawkes had acted under a 'mistaken assumption of unlimited powers', and that had an investigation been made earlier it 'would have probably resulted in the amelioration of the condition under which the internees were then living, and the creation of a situation controlled and conducted more in accordance with what is known in every British community as fair, strict and impartial administration.'[34]

Despite the seriousness of the claims against him, Hawkes seems to have remained impervious to the criticism. There is little sign of contrition in a letter he wrote in August 1916, pleading to be allowed to enlist and regain his commission. He lamented its cancellation after fourteen years of service on the basis of 'conduct likely to cause international complications and reprisals on our own men'. In the light of countless atrocities committed by the enemy, the reason given for the 'unjust treatment' meted out to him seemed 'utterly absurd'. Eventually Hawkes took the path of enlisting in the AIF as a private, was promoted to sergeant and sent to Europe with a unit of the Army Medical Corps. He arrived too late to see action.[35]

If the military had hoped that the cancellation of Hawkes's commission would avoid international repercussions, then its hopes were dashed. The outcomes of the enquiries reached Germany, and reports of the abuses were published in German newspapers. The British Foreign Secretary, Sir Edward Grey, wrote a response to German concerns over incidents at Torrens Island outlining how Hawkes had been punished and requesting information on how perpetrators of abuse in German prisoners of war camps had been prosecuted. Nonetheless, an article appeared in the 13 September 1918 edition of the *Frankfurter Zeitung* under the heading 'Porres, Ireland' a mis-spelling of 'Torrens Island'. The report gave its readers a distorted account of abuses in the camp, stating: 'This vile fellow [Captain Hawkes] shot at a prisoner who asked him for a cigarette, with his revolver, killing an onlooker and wounding another'. It went on to conclude, 'Only through the most severe countermeasures against Australian prisoners in our hands will it be possible to force the barbarous descendants of the former Australian convict state to adopt a humane attitude'.[36] The author might not have been well informed about South Australia's free settler past, but the message was chilling.

INTERNED
Torrens Island 1914-1915

Internees Stefan Pokora, Wilhelm Reinhard, Paul Dubotzki, Ulrich Meier, Leopold Ebner and Walter Emde at Torrens Island internment camp, 1915.

Dubotzki Collection, courtesy Sydney Living Museums

Seven prisoners gathered in front of one of the tents. In the white shirt in the middle, smoking a cigarette, is Paul Dubotzki.

Dubotzki Collection, courtesy Sydney Living Museums

Roll-call, every afternoon at 3 pm. Photograph by Paul Dubotzki.

State Library of New South Wales, MLMSS 261/2/17

Located in the Port River estuary, Torrens Island was subject to flooding at high tide. Photograph by Paul Dubotzki.

State Library of New South Wales, MLMSS 261/2/17

PHOTO
DUBOTZKY

The 'kitchens' were cobbled together by the prisoners using whatever materials they could find. Photograph by Paul Dubotzki.

State Library of New South Wales, MLMSS 261/2/17

Ration distribution. In his caption Paul Dubotzki laments, 'Every day foul mutton and potatoes.' Photograph by Paul Dubotzki.

State Library of New South Wales, MLMSS 261/2/17

Photo
DOBOTZKÝ

Latrine facilities were primitive in the extreme. These men are not seeking to insult the photographer – almost certainly Paul Dubotzki – but performing their daily ablutions. On the back of the image Frank Bungardy has written,

'Convenience facility on Torrens Island. Wood (footboards) noticed bought and payed for by the Internees. 16 new holes each day had to be dug by the Internees and the old used ones covered again with sand. No payment.'

State Library of New South Wales, MLMSS 261/2/17

Collecting firewood. Bungardy noted that two prisoners from each tent set off each morning to find firewood and bring it back to the camp. Photograph by Paul Dubotzki.

National Library of Australia 3792180

PHOTO
DUBOTZKI

Dubotzki's postcard image of men gathering firewood. The caption by Frank Bungardy on the back of the postcard reads, 'Internees gathering their daily firewood under escort on Torrens Isl. S.A. Contradictory to orders a live tree will have to suffer, as no dead wood is to be found. Axes had to be bought by Internees themself, Government suplied none.'

State Library of New South Wales, MLMSS 261/2/17

Photo
DUBOTZKY

One of a number of bands formed by the internees on Torrens Island. Photograph by Paul Dubotzki.

State Library of South Australia, B 9000

The Teutonia Singing Club as photographed by Paul Dubotzki.

State Library of South Australia, B 9001

This is one of the photographs taken by Dubotzki, printed in postcard format, and kept in an album by Frank Bungardy. Bungardy's caption on the back reads, 'Athletic Club, G.C.C. [German Concentration Camp] Torrens Island, July 1915. This wher the only remedy to keep body and mind together to [stay] out of the Luny house.'

State Library of New South Wales, MLMSS 261/2/17

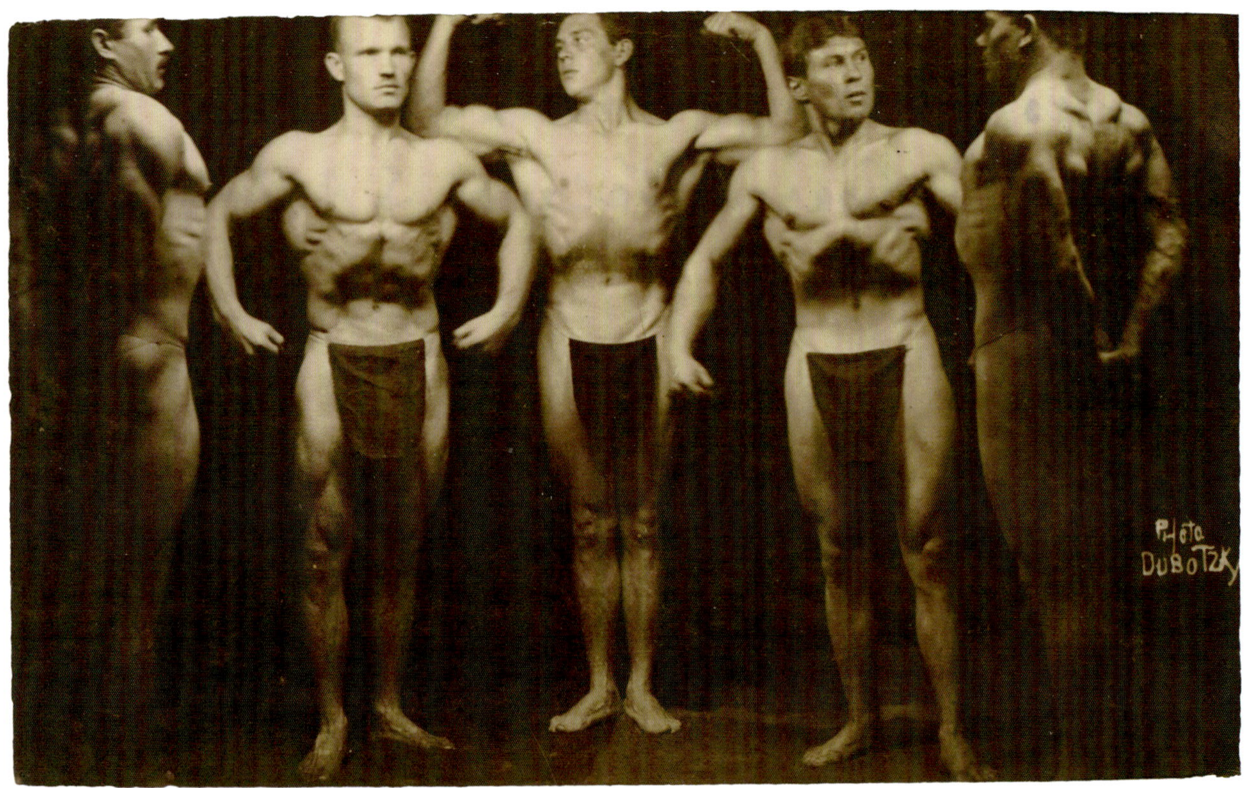


In trying circumstances prisoners did what they could to keep themselves in good physical shape. At least a few of them, as this image by Dubotzki suggests, were remarkably successful. Bungardy noted that the prisoners also formed an athletics and a football club.

National Library of Australia 2296450

Playing chess was another way to pass the time.

State Library of South Australia, B 8999

The Kaiser Café.

National Library of Australia 5017820

Celebration 'inspections' by internees for the Kaiser's birthday, probably 27 January 1915. This double photograph was probably taken by Dubotzki.

State Library of South Australia, B 46799

The court ladies and a court jester gather to celebrate the Kaiser's birthday, probably 27 January 1915.

State Library of South Australia, B 17351

In the all-male world of the prison camp, the sight of a woman was a rarity. On this occasion, the inhabitants of one of the tents make do with one of their number passing himself off – not entirely successfully – as a member of the opposite sex, in a costume made for the Kaiser's birthday celebrations in January 1915. Photograph by Paul Dubotzki.

State Library of South Australia, B 46798

23

Men gather for a religious service among the tents on Torrens Island. Photograph by Paul Dubotzki.

Dubotzki Collection, courtesy Dieter Kamper

Women from Adelaide's Cheer-up Society visited Torrens Island to keep up the morale of the guards. Dubotzki's caption points out Captain Hawkes, centre, describing him as 'the dog of a commandant'. Photograph by Paul Dubotzki.

State Library of South Australia, B 46796

An undated photograph of the prisoners in the Torrens Island camp, musicians with their instruments in the front row. Photograph by Paul Dubotzki.

Dubotzki Collection, courtesy Dieter Kamper

Paul Dubotzki's group photograph of the guards on Torrens Island. He notes that for something like 150 prisoners at the time there were approximately 95 guards. In the middle of the photograph is Captain Hawkes.

Dubotzki Collection, courtesy Dieter Kamper

The detention compound. Dubotzki's own caption for this photograph reads: 'Thirty days of rainy weather these Germans had to spend in this cage with just one warm feed. A "Tommy" took the photo; an enraged German pulled down his trousers.' The detention compound was accessed by a narrow race designed to ensure it was entered in a single file. The prisoners called it the Hotel de Ville, or the sheepyard.

State Library of New South Wales, MLMSS 261/2/17

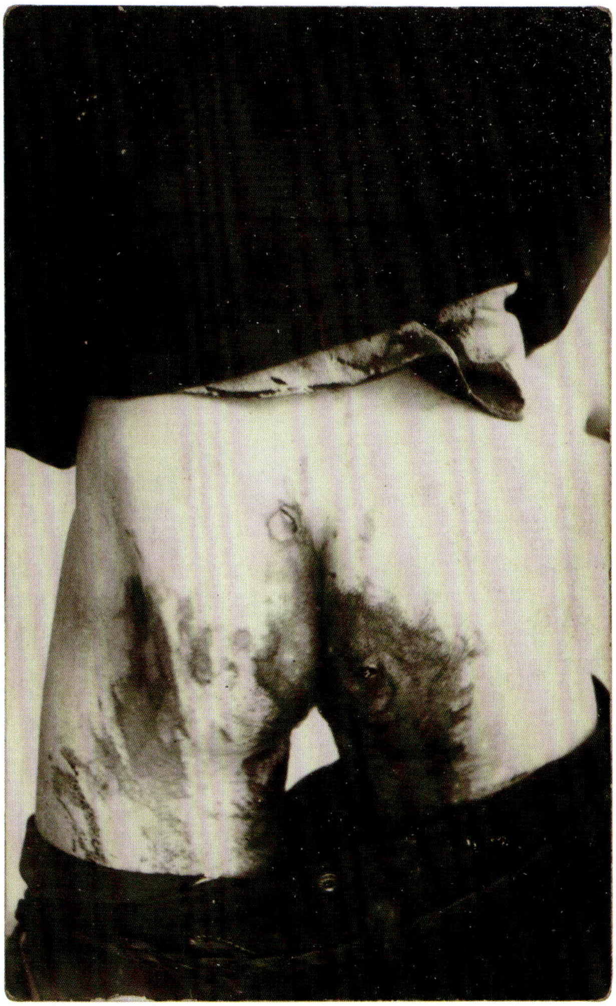

The album of photos accompanying Frank Bungardy's diary contains a number of images of injuries inflicted by a bayonet, taken by Paul Dubotzki, and including this one. Bungardy's caption on the back of the card reads, 'The ill-treatment of a prisoner, 15 stabs in anatomy through a bayonet by a Sergeant. Torrens Island. S.A. July 1915. The black in picture is blood. Stabs distinctly to be seen. Ill-treatment proved without justification, as pris. returned to camp 5 minutes after arrest, being mistaken identity.'

State Library of New South Wales, MLMSS 261/2/17

With the diary recording his internment the boxer Frank Bungardy also kept a number of postcards with photographs, probably taken by Dubotzki. On the back of this postcard, on which Bungardy identifies one particular guard with a cross, Bungardy has written, 'Some of our guards on G.C.C. Torrens Island. S.A. Marked X is the soldier who dealt out the flogging. Private Thiele of Mount Gambier S.A. 4th Military District.' If this is true, then there is more than a hint of irony, since 'Thiele' is a German name.

State Library of New South Wales, MLMSS 261/2/17

Dubotzki's caption on the reverse of this portrait reads: 'This dog was called upon mainly to stick the bayonet into the Germans' soft parts.' Photograph by Paul Dubotzki.

Dubotzki Collection, courtesy Dieter Kamper

# 5. After Torrens Island

This image taken in Holsworthy camp in New South Wales, shows Frank Bungardy to the right of the boxer in the dark shorts.

Australian War Memorial, PO4365.001

The main entrance to the camp at Holsworthy – in those days often spelt Holdsworthy – on the south-western outskirts of Sydney. Most of the internees from Torrens Island were transferred to Holsworthy when Torrens Island was closed in August 1915. The letters above the gate, 'G.C.C.', stand for 'German Concentration Camp'.
Australian War Memorial, PO4970.034

## The camp closes

The Torrens Island Concentration Camp closed on 17 August 1915. At this time there was a consolidation of Australia's internment facilities, as similar camps were shut down in all the states except New South Wales. It is possible that the evidence of the abuse of prisoners might have persuaded authorities to shut that camp down sooner rather than later, but this is not clear. In any case, most of the Torrens internees, some 350 men, were sent to the 'German Concentration Camp' at Holsworthy on the south-western outskirts of Sydney, where an existing camp was expanded to meet the growing demand.

The consolidation of internment in New South Wales had an international dimension, too. Australia was asked by the Colonial Office in London to take 'enemy aliens' from the Straits Settlements (that is, from Singapore and the Malay Peninsula) and Ceylon (today's Sri Lanka), and an agreement was soon reached to this effect. In the next year, 1916, internees from Hong Kong, Fiji and British North Borneo followed.[1] There were efficiencies to be gained, so the logic went, by 'concentrating' these 1200 internees, among them some women and children, with those already behind barbed wire in Australia.

The facility at Holsworthy, sometimes referred to as the 'Liverpool' camp, was much larger than the Torrens Island camp. In its basic features, however, it was similar. At Holsworthy, as on Torrens Island, the military was in control, regulating the daily lives of thousands of Germans and other 'enemy subjects' who, in most cases, were interned for the duration of the war. Although the abuses perpetrated on Torrens

Island seem generally to have been avoided, Holsworthy was not a pleasant place to live, certainly not over a period of months and then years. Accommodation was cramped and rough, boredom and frustration ever present. Many prisoners understandably made appeals for release, but these were granted only in very rare cases.

With row after row of wooden barracks with distinctive canvas awnings, the Holsworthy camp was a much larger facility than Torrens Island, and it was more comfortable – but not much.

Australian War Memorial, H17350

More fortunate prisoners were sent to a camp established at Trial Bay near Kempsey on the northern coast of New South Wales. An abandoned gaol there, located on a rocky headland overlooking the Pacific Ocean, was refitted for its new purpose. The Trial Bay internee population did not reach beyond about 580.[2] They were drawn in large part from the upper echelons of German-Australian and Austrian-Australian society. Among them were businessmen, medical doctors, academics and German consuls. One, for example, was the renowned surgeon Max Herz, another the former Imperial German Consul in Brisbane Eugen Hirschfeld. Paul Dubotzki, the German photographer who had been interned on Torrens Island, was also sent to Trial Bay, of which he left an invaluable photographic record.

There was also a camp at Berrima, some 140 kilometres southwest of Sydney, which remained in existence until the end of the war. It provided a home for officers and crew of ships such as *Scharzfels*, seized in Australian ports during the war, as well as

The Trial Bay camp was generally reserved for more privileged prisoners of higher status. It was located on a picturesque site on the coast near Kempsey in New South Wales. This photograph taken about 1915 shows a view of the bay with guards, camp tents and wooden huts.

Australian War Memorial, P00595.120

a number of German sailors detained in various British colonies. Most of them were merchant seamen, though notable exceptions were the officers and crew of *Emden*, a German warship sunk by the Australian vessel *Sydney* in November 1914. There were some non-sailors, too, in Berrima, but, like Torrens Island and Holsworthy, it was strictly an all-male population.[3]

Trial Bay. Internees play tennis to pass away the time, while dozens of spectators look on.

Dubotzki Collection, courtesy Dieter Kamper

Quite different in character was the 'family camp' at Bourke in western New South Wales, established to cater for the German families brought to Australia from British colonies. These families, numbering fewer than 200 souls, were held together in the Bourke camp until its closure in mid-1918, at which time they were transferred to a similar camp at Molonglo just outside Canberra. Numbers remained small, though they might have grown if authorities had been sympathetic to the appeals of a number of women, who begged for themselves and their children to be interned with their husbands.[4]

The consolidation of the internment system did not mean that the numbers of internees shrank. On the contrary, they grew as the months rolled by, reaching a total of 6890. Most of them – some four and a half thousand – had been residents of the Commonwealth when the war broke out. Those German Australians who eluded the clutches of police and military authorities in the first year of the war could not count on remaining at liberty for the remainder of the war. As much as internment itself, it was the ever-present *threat* of internment that kept the German-Australian population on edge. Meanwhile the New South Wales camps received new internees through to the end of hostilities.[5] Among them were over 200 German South Australians who had not spent any time in the Torrens Island camp but nonetheless became 'prisoners of war', far from family and home, and often without understanding why.

## The home front and the conscription debates

The plight of German Australians through to the end of the war was intimately connected with both the vicissitudes of war on the other side of the world and with the course of domestic politics in Australia.

After the Gallipoli campaign, the focus of Australian military activity shifted to the trenches and battlefields of Europe. Far from offering a respite from the misery of

Turkey, the campaign fought by Australians on the fields of France and Belgium was one of unrelenting privation, hardship, injury and death. Moreover, it was in Europe that the Australians had their first direct contact with German forces. The bloody battles waged at Ypres, Passchendaele and Pozières resulted in significant numbers of Australian casualties.

Back home, the Australian press did not mince its words. Australians and their allies, it was clear, were involved in a life-and-death battle with a brutal and uncompromising enemy.

The federal government took the view that for Australia to prosecute its war effort to the best of its ability, it was necessary to introduce conscription for overseas military service. The Australian constitution dictated that conscription could only be approved if supported in a national referendum. The leading proponent of conscription was Prime Minister Billy Hughes, who pushed his case in a characteristically vigorous and forthright manner. Success would depend very largely on his capacity to persuade Australians that the nation's security was at stake. That meant pointing not only to the dire military situation in Europe, where there was allegedly an urgent need for more Australian troops, but also to the threat at home posed by treacherous 'enemy aliens'.

Hughes had a battle of his own on his hands, because he knew that even in an atmosphere of firm support for the troops already fighting in Europe, there was widespread opposition to the notion that young Australians should be forced against their will into overseas military service. In those circumstances, Hughes played the anti-German card as best he could, hoping to whip up the sort of patriotic fervour which might get his referendum proposal over the line. When the vote was held in October 1916, the 'yes' case put by Hughes and his supporters lost by a narrow margin. Hughes tried again just over a year later, in December of 1917, and once again his proposal was defeated.

Like no other issue, enlistment – whether voluntary or not – tested the loyalties of German Australians. That was so at the very beginning of the war, and it remained the case through the two conscription campaigns. In the first months of the war there were many German Australians who adopted a 'wait-and-see' approach, hesitant to commit their lives to Britain's battle against their ancestral home. For their part, the Australian military authorities, too, were hesitant about enlisting men with German names, and for about the first year of the war young German Australians seeking to enlist were commonly rejected out of hand. Despite all that, it seems that German Australians signed up in numbers proportional to their population in Australia. Some of them, at least, enlisted in the hope that their actions might help their families avoid the ignominy of internment.[6]

## South Australian politics

South Australia's new United Labor Party government under Premier Crawford Vaughan, elected in March 1915, was less sympathetic to South Australia's Germans then the previous government. Vaughan committed himself publicly to doing something about an alleged 'German system of espionage, trickery and bribery'. His declared objective was that 'the German cancer in Australia must be thoroughly rooted out and never allowed to grow again'.[7]

Outside parliament, too, anti-German sentiment was on the rise. One of the vehicles for it was the All-British League, the members of which railed against the German presence in South Australian public life. The views of the league were put vigorously by Charles Allen, a member of its Adelaide branch, when he addressed a gathering of the Port Adelaide branch in July 1916. His topic was 'passive patriotism', and he sought to impress on his audience the need during a time of crisis to 'make a stand in the direction of abolishing German influence'. Allen had some very specific ideas as to how this might be achieved: 'They should take every German J.P.'s name off the list, and should disenfranchise every German, compel every German M.P. to resign his seat, and close up all German schools. (Hear, hear)'.[8]

Allen was followed at the lectern by J.P. Wilson, who, as the *Advertiser* reported, was prepared to go a few steps further in eradicating the German influence:

> In the interests of the State all German influence should be removed from the schools. He wanted all Germans to be disfranchised, and removed from the roll of justices, all Germans unfit for military duty to be immediately deported at their own expense, a special tax levied on all Germans in Australia, and at the end of the war all able-bodied Germans repatriated at their own expense. He would like to see all property accumulated by Germans in Australia confiscated and sold, and all German officers and men removed from passenger and cargo boats, trading in Australian waters. (Applause.) He wanted all persons of German birth and parentage to the third generation of Australian-born disallowed ownership of land in Australia, and that all persons of German birth be classed as German colonists, and treated as prohibited immigrants.[9]

The league was a force to be reckoned with. Its membership was open to men, women and children from the age of twelve; fifteen of its number were also members of parliament. With branches throughout urban and rural South Australia, it was able to use its clout to gather a petition with 49,000 signatures urging immediate and far-reaching action against Germans in the community. The objects of the petition were to disenfranchise persons of enemy origin, to remove such persons from the rolls of justices of the peace, to bar enemy persons from official positions, replacing them with British people, and to close German schools.[10]

In such a highly charged atmosphere, it was little wonder that these views soon had political consequences. In 1916 the Vaughan government passed legislation to close Lutheran primary schools. In the middle of the following year 49 such schools, which were in effect German schools, were taken over by the Minister for Education.[11]

German clubs, too, fell victim to anti-German sentiment, while the German press fared no better. Under the *War Precautions Act* it was forbidden to publish anything in the German language, so South Australia's weekly German-language newspaper *Die Australische Zeitung* had to close. The Lutheran church's publications, too, came to an end, at least until an adjustment could be made and they appeared in English.[12]

Through all of this there were voices of protest and dissent, yet they were powerless to reverse the tide of anti-German sentiment. One of them was the Reverend John Blacket, who turned to the press to register his disgust with the members of the All-British League and their ilk. He wrote,

> Once more, as a true Britisher, I enter my protest against the pesty, spiteful and indiscriminate persecution of people who are as innocent of this diabolical war, as are the members of the so-called 'All-British League'. The conduct of those who are leading an indiscriminate crusade against all our German colonists reminds me of the 'Jew-baiting' that was common on the Continent not many years ago . . . I know a German husband and wife who have given to this war three sons, two of whom will never return.[13]

## The Nomenclature Act

One of the longer lasting consequences of anti-German sentiment in South Australia related to place names. In 1916 the government decided to alter the names of towns and districts in South Australia which suggested a connection with an enemy state. Debate in parliament was launched by W.D. Ponder, who drew attention to recent German crimes perpetrated in the course of the war, among them the sinking of the passenger vessel *Lusitania* and the murder of the British nurse Edith Cavell. The outcome of the debate was a resolution, passed in early August 1916, that names of enemy origin should be replaced with names of British or South Australian origin. To this end, a 'Nomenclature Committee' was formed to present recommendations for approval.

The committee did its work thoroughly, and by 7 November was able to present its report. Though it was well aware that alterations would cause a good deal of confusion, it nonetheless proposed that German names be changed. In many cases the committee proposed that Indigenous names be adopted in the place of German ones. However, in accordance with the fervently pro-British mood of the times, when the changes came into effect in 1918, the outcome was commonly the choice of unambiguously British names. In the case, for example of the village of 'New Mecklenburg', the Nomenclature Committee suggested it be replaced with 'Putpayerta', the Aboriginal name for the district. Archibald Peake, however, who was premier again from July 1917, insisted on 'Gomersal', the name of the Yorkshire town in which his father was born. Similarly, 'Neukirch' in the view of the committee should have been renamed 'Pangarinda', but under Peake's influence it became 'Dimchurch', the English birthplace of his mother.[14]

So it was that 'Hahndorf' became 'Ambleside', 'Blumberg' became 'Birdwood', 'Petersburg' became 'Peterborough', and 'Klemzig' became 'Gaza'. Altogether 69 names were changed. In 1935, and then in the 1970s and 1980s some of the original names were restored, but much of the distinctively German character of the map of South Australia was lost.

Other changes, too, were symptomatic of war-time xenophobia. The pastry known as the 'Berliner Pfannkuchen' was renamed the Kitchener Bun in honour of Britain's secretary of state for war. Many of the German businesses dotted through Adelaide and other parts of the state were forced to close as customers took their patronage elsewhere. One of the victims of commercial discrimination was Carl Stratmann's confectionery business in Beehive Corner. As early as 1915 Stratmann sold his business – along with its medieval German knights – to Haigh's.

## Internment

The changing of names and closing of German schools and businesses were mere inconveniences compared with the profound disruptions suffered by many German Australians in the period after the camp at Torrens Island closed. Most of those men already held on Torrens Island were transferred to New South Wales, but then others fell victim to the heightened levels of suspicion and distrust and were interned. For their families, too, the absence of a breadwinner, and the uncertainty over when he might be returned to the family fold, caused severe hardship.

Some of the new internees were victims of the tightened *War Precautions Act* Regulations. With the rationale that the national interest was at stake, the powers of the Minister for Defence were extended 'to cover the internment of disloyal natural born [that is, Australian-born] subjects of enemy descent, and of persons of hostile origin or association'. Paragraph 56a of the regulations could be used against anyone who had contact with an 'enemy alien', and by October of 1916 the regulations applied to 'all aliens, whether enemy or otherwise'. Moreover, those who found themselves in internment because of the application of the extended regulations could expect to stay there for a very long time. There was no recourse to an independent review process or an avenue of judicial appeal.[15]

For a fortunate few, internment was relatively brief, and in South Australia. In these instances the site of internment was Fort Largs, built in the late nineteenth century to defend Port Adelaide from seaborne attack. For others, Fort Largs was a provisional but grim holding place, until transport to New South Wales, and longer-term internment, could be arranged. Among these internees were just under 20 who were naturalised and another group numbering just over 20 who were natural-born British subjects, that is, Australians of German descent. They were interned because the Minister for Defence had issued a 'Minister's Warrant'.

Often it was not at all clear to the internees just why it was that they found themselves behind barbed wire, hundreds of kilometres from their families. As the process was largely opaque, they could only speculate. Almost certainly there were instances where internment was the result of disagreements among neighbours, petty feuding, business rivalries or simply a visceral anti-German prejudice.

Some of the Germans who became victims of the rising tensions were men of high profile. One of them was the German consul in Adelaide, Hugo Carl Emil Muecke, who had called Governor Sir Henry Galway on the morning that Australia entered the war. Born in Germany in 1842, he came to Adelaide as a young boy aboard *Princess Louise*. He was naturalised in 1866. Muecke was a German speaker, but by the time of the outbreak of the First World War he was the only member of his family who was. In the years leading to the war he established himself as a pillar of South

Australian society – among other offices he had been a member of the Legislative Council and Justice of the Peace. He was also a prominent businessman, member of the Adelaide Chamber of Commerce, Freemason and a member of the German Club. Nonetheless, when war was declared, accusations of disloyalty were levelled at him. He turned to the press to make it known that he disapproved of Germany's conduct of the war, and that his own son, having served at Gallipoli, was now with British forces in France. In the end, none of this helped, and in April 1916 he was interned at Fort Largs. After appeals were lodged by sympathetic businessmen, he was released from the fort but still held in detention in his own home in Medindie.[16]

The internees and their families could lodge requests for release with the military authorities, but records indicate that these were very rarely successful. Where dependants of internees suffered obvious economic hardship, an allowance was paid which allowed them to feed themselves for the duration of hostilities. Many committed what money they had to supporting themselves for as long as they could, but the drain on their savings and the damage done to family businesses meant that they suffered the consequences of the male breadwinner's internment long into the post-war period. That applies to those who remained in Australia and also to those who were sent to Germany, where economic circumstances in the aftermath of the war remained dire for years to come.

In 1918 it gradually became clear that the war was approaching an end, and that the Central Powers would be defeated. Australian forces played an important role in securing a number of victories on the Western Front. From May of 1918 the commander of the Australian Corps on the Western Front was John Monash. The son of German Jewish immigrants to Australia, and a fluent German-speaker himself, Monash was the architect of a series of remarkable successes in battles against German forces in north-western France. His prominent role in Europe might have helped ensure that circumstances did not deteriorate further for German Australians back home.

On the other hand, those circumstances did not improve, even with victory in sight. The great majority of internees remained behind wire until the end of the war, and then for several months beyond as well.

## After the war

The guns of Europe fell silent on 11 November 1918, when the armistice was signed. The war had ended, yet the frustration continued for those who were now Australia's 'ex-enemy aliens'. Some internees were released – mainly naturalised and natural-born British subjects against whom there was little evidence of disloyalty, as well as some long-standing residents who had volunteered for internment.[17] But for most there would be months of anxiety and uncertainty before their future was determined.

The fate that awaited most was repatriation. That was uncontroversial enough for people like August Strycker and the officers of *Scharzfels*. They were among those who, in August 1914, had been caught in the wrong place at the wrong time and were eager to rejoin family and friends back in Germany just as soon as they could.

More vexed, however, was the question of what would become of those who had lived in Australia before the war, in some cases for very long periods. The range of hopes among them was wide. Some simply wished to return to their families in various parts of Australia as soon as they possibly could. Others were so disgusted with the manner in which they had been treated that they could barely wait for the opportunity to leave Australia behind and return to Europe. That might have meant Germany, but it could also have meant Austria, Yugoslavia or Poland. The map of Europe had been redrawn, and much of the continent still displayed the open wounds of war.

In the end, the preferences of the internees counted for little. The Australian Government would decide their fate, taking advice from a body it established under the name 'Aliens Committee'. Even months after victory was secured, the strong preference in the majority of cases was for repatriation, even when internees voiced a desire to remain in Australia. The lists of those to be repatriated extended even to people who were not interned but who, military intelligence officials determined, would pose a risk if they remained in Australia. In theory internees could appeal against repatriation, and tribunals were established to hear such appeals, but only in 127 cases did the tribunals find in favour of the interned 'ex-enemy aliens'. Most of the South Australian Germans who had been naturalised before the war were released on parole at war's end; a handful were among those repatriated to Germany. Similarly, those born in South Australia of German descent who had found themselves behind barbed wire were also released on parole. The disaffected among them were of course at liberty to leave Australia at their own expense.[18]

The first to be deported were those who left voluntarily, dismayed that the process could not begin until May of 1919. The last to board ships bound for Europe were those who had lodged appeals; most of them had left Australia by September of that year, but the process continued into 1920. Altogether 6150 people made the journey back to Europe. The great majority of them – 5414 – had been vegetating in places like the Torrens Island and Holsworthy camps for years. The rest were either family members or ex-enemy aliens who had not been interned but had offered – or been ordered – to leave the country.[19]

The photographer Paul Dubotzki was one of those to leave Australia aboard *Kursk*. Here he captures a scene of passengers huddled together on deck.

Dubotzki Collection, courtesy Dieter Kamper

German immigrants were unwelcome in Australia for some years after the war, such was the durability of anti-German sentiment. In time, however, there were those among the unwillingly deported who made their way back to Australia. It was a bold move, based on a willingness on their part to put the wartime past behind them, and a hope that Australians might do the same. In this way some were able to rebuild their lives successfully in the years that followed, until the outbreak of another war threw up the issue of their loyalty all over again.

Among the deported were the two men who had gone to great lengths to document the time they spent in the camp on Torrens Island. Dubotzki left aboard *Kursk* in May, returning to Germany to resume his career as a photographer. Frank Bungardy, the boxer from Broken Hill, was deported aboard *Valencia* in October 1919. Back in Germany he would return to the boxing ring, at least for a while. By the time the two men passed through Sydney Heads, the months they had spent on Torrens Island were already just a memory. Nonetheless, it was one they would never forget.

# Bulgarians

On 14 October 1915 Bulgaria entered the war on the side of the Central Powers. At that time Australia's Bulgarian population numbered at most a few hundred, who were now regarded as 'enemy aliens' in Australia.

In South Australia there was a small population of Bulgarians employed in the mining industry. In November 1915 a military force was sent from Adelaide to arrest Bulgarian men in both Port Pirie and Hummock's Hill (later Whyalla). According to a newspaper report from the time, the Bulgarians' departure attracted much local interest:

> A large crowd gathered at the Ellen street station to see the departure of the captives. They occupied one of the large double carriages, and the platforms were guarded by armed sentries. The captives appeared to be in good spirits. Some of their friends purchased for them fruit and many bottles of temperance drinks while the train remained in the street.

Forty-four Bulgarians were interned on 13 November 1915; another three were already being held. By this time the Torrens Island camp was closed, and they were soon transferred to Holsworthy camp in New South Wales. After an agreement was struck between the governments of Britain and Bulgaria in March 1916, the Bulgarians were released from internment. According to official figures, this change of policy affected 47 Bulgarians from the 4th Military District. Upon their release many chose to make their way back to Port Pirie. Their arrival there was reported to have been greeted with 'indignation' by local workers.

# The Dechert Brothers

In the language of the time, all four of the Dechert brothers – Albert Waldemar Rupert (23), Friedrich Theodor Julius (27), Wilhelm Johann Georg (27) and Carl Friedrich Wilhelm Dechert (34) – were 'Natural Born British Subjects'. Their place of birth was Angaston, South Australia, but by the time of the war all lived in Norwood, and all were public servants. Until 1916 they were probably best known in Adelaide for their performances on the tennis court.

That all changed when the brothers made it known in October 1916 that they would not enlist in the AIF to fight against their father's homeland. A response of indignation was immediate and widespread. Their refusals to enlist were taken as signs of disloyalty. Even Prime Minister Billy Hughes weighed into the Dechert controversy: 'The call of the blood was too strong for them to resist. We Britons in times of peace have been foolishly credulous, opening the gates of our inmost citadels to Germans, taking their hypocritical protestations of friendship at their face value'. The *Adelaide Mail* concurred. The behaviour of the Decherts was 'an outrageous crime against the community'.

All the Dechert brothers resigned their positions, but worse was soon to follow for them. It was on a 'Minister's Warrant' – issued by the Minister for Defence – that all the brothers were arrested on 26 October and interned, initially at Fort Largs and then Holsworthy.

These events occurred at a peculiarly sensitive time on the Australian home front. On 28 October the first of two referendums on conscription was held. Billy Hughes campaigned with huge vigour in favour of it – and lost narrowly.

Albert Waldemar Rupert Dechert became the secretary of the Association of Natural Born Subjects, an organisation that fought to protect the rights of those who were bitterly disillusioned by the contempt with which the country of their birth was treating them.

Records show that all the Decherts were 'released unconditionally' from Holsworthy on 13 February 1919. Yet the story has an interesting postscript. At the end of 1926 an Adelaide newspaper carried a notice that Friedrich Julius Dechert, father of eight children, had died in Berlin on 27 December of that year.

The Australian-born Dechert brothers, internees at Holsworthy in New South Wales.

NAA: D3597 Album of identification photographs of enemy aliens (civilian and prisoner of war) interned at Liverpool Camp, NSW during World War I

# Leopold Ebner

Leopold Ebner was one of the Austrians interned on Torrens Island. He had come to Australia in 1908 as a seventeen-year-old. He worked as a gardener for an elderly German couple, the Roesners, in Crafers.

Leopold Ebner, photographed by Paul Dubotzki [detail of group image].

Dubotzki Collection, courtesy Sydney Living Museums

In February 1915 Ebner was arrested on suspicion of having sabotaged a telegraph line. The accusation was levelled at him, without proof, by the local policeman, Senior Constable John Opie. Ebner was released from Torrens Island in August 1915 when the Roesners provided a bond on his behalf.

Opie's suspicions remained undiluted, and in August 1916 the policeman gave renewed voice to his concern that Ebner 'may need watching', though he still could not provide any evidence of disloyal conduct by Ebner. Nonetheless, in response to the policeman's suspicions, Ebner was persuaded to surrender his parole, and in so doing he relieved the Roesners of their responsibility for him.

Ebner was sent to the Holsworthy camp, from where he pleaded on numerous occasions for his release. Not until January 1919 was his wish finally granted; he was paroled and made his way back to South Australia. There he learned that his father in Austria was gravely ill. Told that 'enemy aliens' were still not permitted to leave the country, he applied for, and was granted, repatriation. Alas, he arrived in Austria too late to see his father, who had passed away a few months earlier. His long voyage had been in vain. Australian authorities then blocked his efforts to return to Australia on the grounds that he had been repatriated to his homeland and Australia did not seek immigrants from its former enemies.

## Carl Ernst

Carl Ernst was one of many Germans in the region of Loxton who crossed swords with the local policeman Richard Alfred Lenthall. His arrest and internment exemplify the coordination of police and military authorities in the internment of 'enemy aliens'.

Ernst was born in Germany in 1871, arrived in Australia in 1889 and married an Australian woman, with whom he had eight children. He was not among those interned on Torrens Island, but he eventually found himself in trouble with the law – and behind barbed wire.

In September 1915 Constable Lenthall reported that he found no evidence for Ernst's claim that he had been naturalised and that he had not been reporting to the police as required. Lenthall wrote to his superior in Adelaide to enquire if he should arrest Ernst for making false claims about his naturalisation and for failing to report on parole. In response to the police enquiry, the military authorities ordered Ernst's arrest and internment. He was held for a short time – possibly at Keswick – and then paroled.

This proved a temporary reprieve, in large part due to the intervention of a certain Andrew Russell Snodgrass, a neighbour of Ernst, who lodged a complaint about the German's behaviour. According to Snodgrass, he had encountered Ernst one day in April 1916, when Ernst was returning from the butcher's shop he kept in Loxton – having possibly had a drink or two. Ernst allegedly made malicious, slanderous remarks about both Snodgrass and his wife, and expressed hostility to Britain and a loyalty to Germany. So heated did their meeting become, according to Snodgrass, that verbal turned to physical abuse.

In June 1916 Ernst was arrested and interned at Largs Bay, and from there he was taken to the Holsworthy camp. It is likely that Snodgrass's denunciation of him played a key role. Ernst denied the allegations made against him, though he did not deny that hostility had arisen between the two men. The cause, in his view, was Snodgrass's failure to return machinery that Ernst had lent him. A neighbourly spat, it seems, put Ernst behind barbed wire for the next three years.

Forced to leave his wife and children to fend for themselves, Ernst was considered for repatriation to Germany after the war, but was spared that fate and returned home in September 1919. The war might have been long over, but he was still required to report regularly to the police.

In time Ernst applied again for naturalisation, but without success.

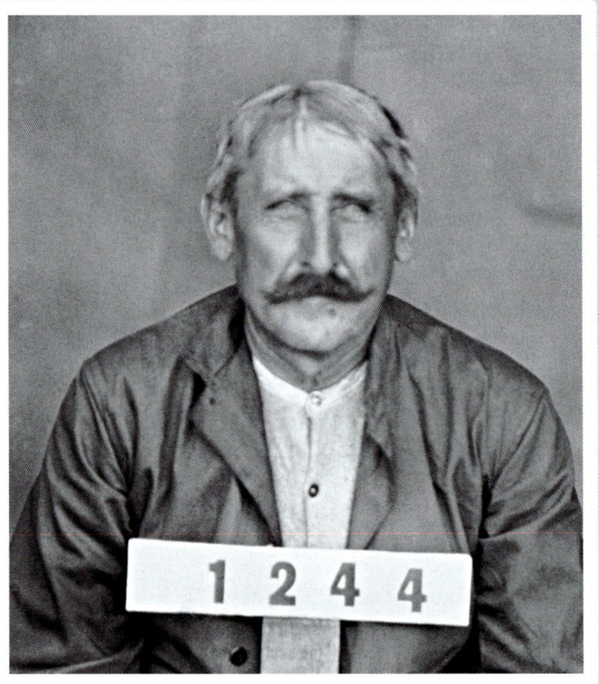


Carl Ernst during his internment at Holsworthy.

NAA: D3597 1244, Ernst, Karl

PRISONERS OF WAR
DATE 18.9.15
REGISTRY No. 424

Police Station Loxton
Sept 13th 1915

Re Carl Ernst

Sir

I have the honor to report for your information that a German Subject named Carl Ernst who has resided in the Loxton district for over 7 years and was born in Westfallen Germany has never reported himself and has not been paroled

I have asked him on two different occasions if he was naturalized and he said "Yes." but since he he has been compelled to fill in a 'War Census' card I have ascertained that he is not naturalized and has stated on the card that he is not naturalized.

Ernst is a married man residing in Hd of Pyap about 16 miles from Loxton, and I respectfully request to be directed if this man is to be arrested and interned.

To
Inspector Bushell
Police Barracks
Adelaide

I have the honor to be
Sir
Your obedient Servant
R.A. Lenthall
M. Constable

No Record of Ernst. DG

Mounted Constable Lenthall wrote to his superior in Adelaide to report that Ernst had not registered and ask if Ernst should be arrested and interned.

NAA: D1915 SA262, Ernst, Carl – Pyap, near Loxton, SA – disloyalty and internment

PRISONERS OF WAR
DATE
REGISTRY No. 424

Pyap S.A.
1st May 1919.

The Commandant
4th Military District
Keswick. Adelaide

Dear Sir

re Carl Ernst. Internee Liverpool N.S.W.

We the undersigned request that the above Internee's case be considered, and that he be liberated in Australia and be allowed to rejoin his family whom we know to be careful industrious people, of good repute.

Trusting that our request will receive your consideration

We are dear Sir
Yours faithfully

H. S. Le Page — Pyap
Bruce H. Laffer — Agent & Secretary Loxton
A.H. Limbert — Trader. Loxton.
A.H. Landseer Bt. — Merchant
G.S. Williams — Manager
[illegible] — Loxton S.A.
B. Halkett — Loxton.
H.A. Wedd — Loxton.
B.T.H. Cox — Pyap

As Ernst faced the possibility of deportation, a number of his acquaintances write in support of his return to Pyap.

NAA: D1915 SA262, Ernst, Carl – Pyap, near Loxton, SA – disloyalty and internment

# Hermann Carl Goers

Hermann Carl Goers was born in Australia and lived in Tanunda, where he was the owner and publisher of the *Barossa News*. He was interned in the Holsworthy camp in May 1916. The hardships caused by his absence led his wife Ottilie to write to the military authorities at Keswick Barracks:

> Will you please give me a weekly allowance of ten shillings for my daughter and me, since my husband was sent to Liverpool in 22 May 1916. We have tried to continue in our home, as my husband's wages were stopped once he was taken away from us. I am nearly 50 years of age and cannot earn anything.

In August 1918 Goers was still in Holsworthy, and in a letter to his daughter Nora in South Australia he could not contain his frustration at his ongoing internment:

> Here I am well in the third year in this most damnable camp and God knows how much longer I shall have to remain here and why? God will punish these culprits who made those strong statements against me, and this is what they call justice and fair play, freedom and liberty. I would not have believed it had I not seen it for myself. It will never be forgotten and forgiven, no, never.

Goers was finally released on parole on 11 September 1919. In the next war, however, he once more attracted the attention of authorities. A security report on him noted, 'Born in Australia, he still clings to the German language and ideas and is just another Australian born German who prefers to be faithful to the country he has never seen than to the country of his livelihood and birth'.

## Karl Wilhelm Lude

Karl Wilhelm Lude was one of many Germans from the Loxton district interned on Torrens Island, arrested by the Loxton Mounted Constable Richard Alfred Lenthall. Lude, a butcher by trade, was born in Germany and migrated to Australia in 1908. In June 1914, just a couple of months before the outbreak of war, he married an Australian-born woman, Hulda Paulena Milich. Just after the outbreak of war, in September 1914, Lude lodged an unsuccessful application for naturalisation.

At that time he was on parole, but he was arrested on 27 October 1914, having been accused of threatening to kill Lenthall. Lude was interned at Keswick Barracks and then transferred to Torrens Island.

When the Torrens Island camp was closed in August 1915, Lude was transferred to Holsworthy in New South Wales. At the end of the war he was repatriated, leaving behind his wife and child still living in South Australia. Soon after leaving Australia on *Valencia* in 1919, Lude made his way to Java, where his wife and child joined him in 1921. Pregnant once more, Hulda Paulena Lude returned – quite legally – to her parents in South Australia to give birth. Karl Wilhelm made his way back to Australia illegally as a stowaway. Eventually he was permitted to stay permanently and was granted the naturalisation denied him in 1914. The Ludes chose to settle in Brisbane, not back in Loxton.

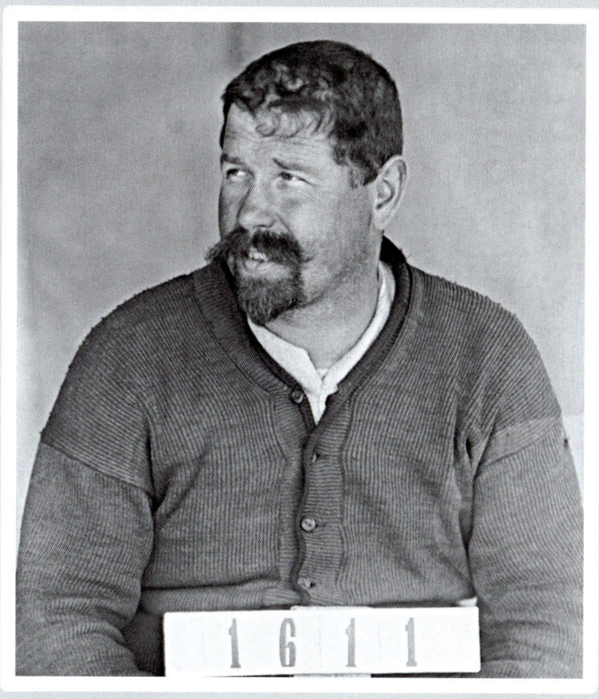


Karl Wilhelm Lude after his transfer from Torrens Island to the Holsworthy camp.

NAA: D3597 1611, Lude, Karl

# John Tossold

John Tossold in Holsworthy, New South Wales.

NAA: 3597, 5369, Tosold, Johann

John, or Johann, Tossold (or Tosold) was a man of some mystery. Depending on which records are consulted, he was born in Bichl in the Russian part of Poland, in Krakow in the Austrian part of Poland, in Graz in the Styrian region of Austria, or in the Austrian capital Vienna. His year of birth was 1870, or perhaps 1874. After entry into Australia in 1905 Tossold worked as a labourer. By 1914 he lived and worked in Cleve. Like many 'enemy aliens' he applied unsuccessfully for naturalisation after the outbreak of war.

On 24 July 1915 he was arrested under the direction of military authorities and interned at Fort Largs, but he claimed to be a naturalised US citizen and was released on 8 October 1915. Later it was established that he held only a 'certificate of intention to become naturalised in the USA'.

On 12 May 1917, still purporting to be a naturalised American, he enlisted in the AIF. By this time the USA had entered the war against Germany. Australian authorities came to the view that Tossold's enlistment was merely a ploy by Tossold to get out of the country. By early June he had been discharged and then re-interned as a prisoner of war.

After the war Tossold was repatriated, but he was back in Australia with a young wife and two children in 1927, armed with a Landing Permit. However, the application for naturalisation he lodged in 1932 was turned down. It was noted that he had been interned during the First World War and had allegedly been 'very disloyal in his attitude towards the British Empire'. A third application for naturalisation, lodged after the Second World War, was successful.

# Heinrich von Zülow

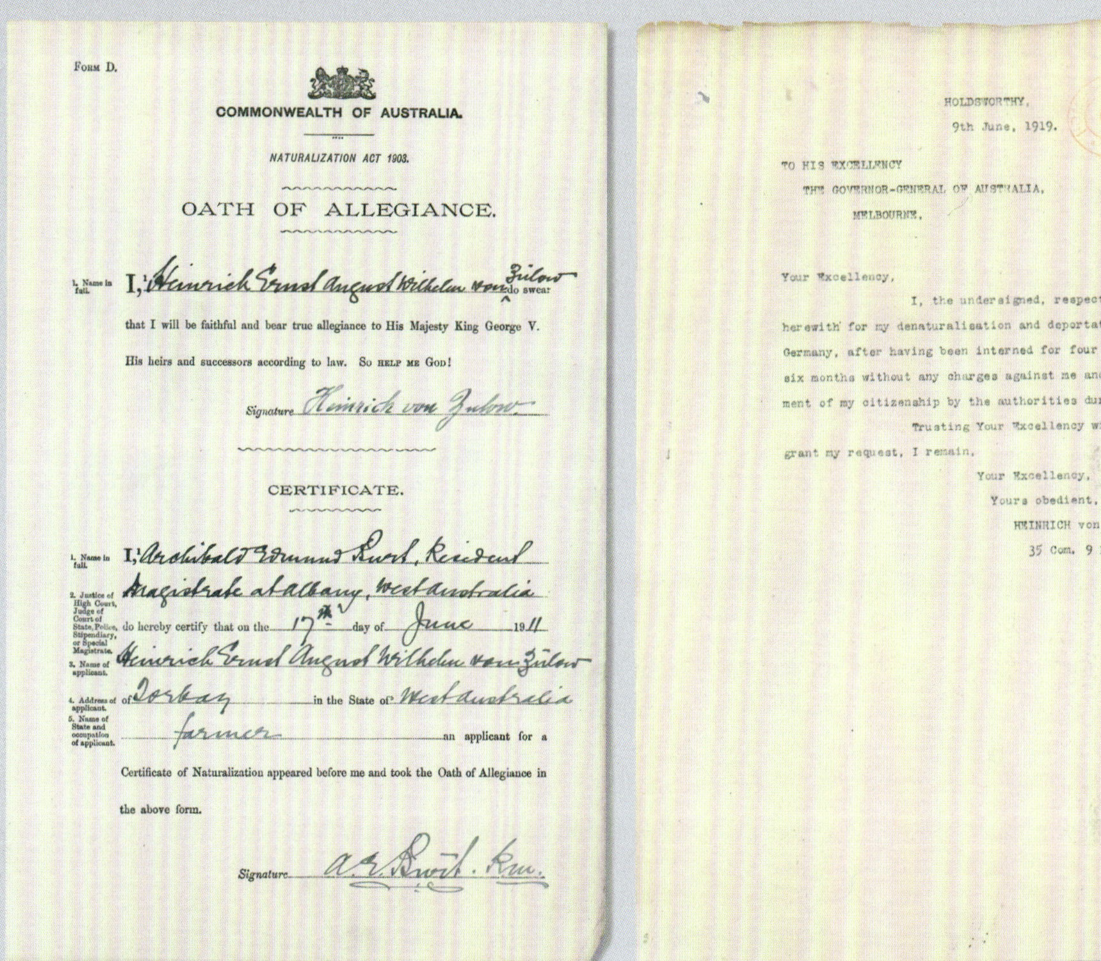

Form D.

COMMONWEALTH OF AUSTRALIA.

NATURALIZATION ACT 1903.

OATH OF ALLEGIANCE.

1. Name in full. I,[1] Heinrich Ernst August Wilhelm von Zülow do swear that I will be faithful and bear true allegiance to His Majesty King George V. His heirs and successors according to law. So help me God!

Signature Heinrich von Zülow

CERTIFICATE.

1. Name in full. I,[1] Archibald Edmund Burt, Resident
2. Justice of High Court, Judge of Court of State, Police, Stipendiary, or Special Magistrate. Magistrate at Albany, West Australia do hereby certify that on the 17th day of June 1911
3. Name of applicant. Heinrich Ernst August Wilhelm von Zülow
4. Address of applicant. of Torbay in the State of West Australia
5. Name of State and occupation of applicant. farmer an applicant for a Certificate of Naturalization appeared before me and took the Oath of Allegiance in the above form.

Signature A. E. Burt. R.M.

HOLDSWORTHY,
9th June, 1919.

09004

TO HIS EXCELLENCY
THE GOVERNOR-GENERAL OF AUSTRALIA,
MELBOURNE.

Your Excellency,

I, the undersigned, respectfully beg herewith for my denaturalisation and deportation to Germany, after having been interned for four years and six months without any charges against me and no acknowledgment of my citizenship by the authorities during the war.

Trusting Your Excellency will kindly grant my request, I remain,

Your Excellency,
Yours obedient,
HEINRICH von ZULOW
35 Com. 9 Mess.

Heinrich von Zülow's Oath of Allegiance to King George V.

NAA: A1 1919/14799 Heinrich Ernst Augustus Wilhelm Von Zulow, Naturalisation

From inside the Holsworthy camp, seven months after the conclusion of the war, von Zülow requests the revocation of his naturalisation and his deportation to Germany.

NAA: A1 1919/14799 Heinrich Ernst Augustus Wilhelm Von Zulow, Naturalisation

The Saxon-born farmer Heinrich Ernst August Wilhelm von Zülow, a prisoner on Torrens Island and then in Holsworthy, was one of those who had been naturalised before the war, in his case in Western Australia in 1911. He had, by then, been living in Australia some six years. As part of that process he had taken an Oath of Allegiance. He had surrendered himself for internment on Torrens Island because he was destitute. At the end of the war he saw no reason to wish to remain in Australia, as he explained in his letter to the Governor-General.

# Notes

## 1. SS *Scharzfels*

1 *Daily Herald,* 6 August 1914, p. 5.

2 *Chronicle,* 8 August 1914, p. 38; *Register,* 6 August 1914, p. 8; *Mail*, 7 August 19 14, p. 3.

3 *Daily Herald*, 28 November 1914, p. 6.

4 *Daily Herald*, 30 September 1914, p. 5.

5 *Daily Herald,* 1 December 1914, p. 6.

6 *Register,* 17 November 1914, p. 6.

7 *Register,* 3 December 1914, p. 5.

## 2. German South Australia

1 Lodewyckx, p. 246.

2 Fischer, 'Integration', p. 8.

## 3. Interned

1 *Advertiser,* 30 June 1914, p. 9.

2 Scott, p. 6, 21; Day p. 288.

3 *Advertiser,* 30 July 1914, p. 14; *Register,* 29 July 1914, p. 5.

4 *Advertiser*, 31 July 1914, p. 8.

5 Scott, p. 22.

6 Ibid. p. 22.

7 Ibid. p. 11; Day, p. 289.

8 *Register*, 5 August 1914, p. 10.

9 Parliamentary Debates South Australia (Hansard), 1914, Twenty-First Parliament, Fourth Session, p. 210.

10 Ibid. p. 212, 214, 217; *Advertiser,* 5 August 1914, p. 15–17.

11 Scott, p. 14; *Advertiser,* 6 August 1914, p. 8.

12 *Advertiser*, 6 August 1914, p. 8.

13 Parliamentary Debates South Australia (Hansard), 1914, Twenty-First Parliament, Fourth Session, p. 218, 217.

14 *Advertiser,* 6 August 1914, p. 8.

15 Ibid. p. 10. The report began with the observation that similar scenes had not been seen since the South African war.

16 Ibid. For an account of a strikingly similar scene in Petersburg (Peterborough from 1917) see *Petersburg Times*, 7 August, 1914, p. 3.

17 *Advertiser*, 6 August 1914, p. 10.

18 *Register*, 6 August 1914, p. 6.

19 *Advertiser*, 11 August 1914, p. 10; Scott, p. 109.

20 Fischer, *Enemy Aliens,* p. 74.

21 Morton, p. 9, 29; Scott, p. 114.

22 *Advertiser*, 7 December 1914, p. 10; figures based on analysis of the files NAA: D2286, Nominal roll of prisoners of war interned at Torrens Island concentration camp 1915, and NAA: A367 C18000 Part 1, War Internees and Deportees 1914–1919.

23 Scott, p. 60–66.

24 Ibid. p. 41; Morton, p. 283.

25 Ibid. p. 14.

26 Ibid. p. 196.

27 McKernan, p. 166; Fischer, *Enemy Aliens*, p. 102.

28 Williams, p. 57.

29 Morton, p. 383. Note that the section previously No. 26 was re-numbered 55; this new section was No. 56.

30 Morton notes that a total of 61 natural-born British subjects were interned in Australia during the First World War, p. 355.

31 Ibid. p. 92–95; Scott, p. 112.

32 Fischer, *Enemy Aliens*, p. 81. Based on stated reasons for internment, nominal roll II, NAA: D2286, Nominal roll of prisoners of war interned at Torrens Island concentration camp 1915. Note that Morton concludes that a 'substantial minority' of internees fall into this category: Morton, p. 133.

33 Morton, p. 101.

34 Bungardy, p. 42, 58–59.

35 Morton, p. 102.

The Bavarian Band *Daily Herald,* 15 January 1915, p. 4.

Broken Hill Stephen Thompson, '1915 Broken Hill Ottoman Flag', http://www.migrationheritage.nsw.gov.au/exhibition/objectsthroughtime/broken-hill-ottoman-flag; 'Memorabilia 1915', *Register*, 31 December 1915, p. 8; 'Aliens from Broken Hill', *Chronicle*, 9 Jan 1915, p. 46; NAA: MP1565/2 List of prisoners of war captured and interned in Australia.

Theodor Dudic (or Tom Dudich) NAA: D1915, SA444, Dudich, Theodore [or Theodor Duduc or Teodor Dudics] – Melbourne – application for naturalization; NAA: MP16/1 1915/3/759, DUDICH, Theodore.

Georg Paul Fischer NAA: D1915 SA 2176, FISCHER Georg Paul – naturalisation.

Johann Gerdes NAA: D1915, SA21651, GERDES Johann; NAA: B78 1955/GERDES Johann – Nationality: German – Arrived Adelaide per Alpena May 1914.

Max Hemmerdinger NAA: A711/4203 Hemmerdinger, Max – Memorial of Naturalisation; 'Patriotic Germans at Eudunda', *Register*, 26 February 1900 p. 5; NAA: A367 C18000 PART 1 War Internees and Deportees 1914–1919; NAA D2286 Vols 1 & 2, Nominal Roll; NAA: A711 4203.

Theodor August Joseph Kleine NAA: D3597 4282 KLEINE, Theodor; NAA: MP367/1 item 567/7/2687 'Release of Internees – Fourth List'; Richard James Morton, 'The enemy within the gates: the internment of Australian citizens during the Great War', doctoral thesis, La Trobe University, 1990, p. 103.

Alois Hosch NAA: MP1565/2, List of prisoners of War Captured and Interned in Australia; NAA: D1915 SA938, Hosch, Alois [prisoner of war (internee)]; application for naturalisation.

Loxton 'The Last of Loxton. Commission's Detailed Report', *Mail,* 17 April 1920, p. 2.

Anton Peter Matulovich NAA: D1915 SA1270, MATULOVICH, Anton, Enquiry by Public Trustee.

Martin Trojan Martin Trojan, *Hinter Stein und Stacheldraht. Australische Schattenbilder*, Bremen: Carl Schünemann n. d., p. 221–22.

The War Precautions Act *Commonwealth Parliamentary Debates (CPD)*, Senate, 28 Oct 1914, p. 342, 375, 372; *Lloyd v Wallach* [1915] High Court of Australia 60.

## 4. Torrens Island Concentration Camp

1 Bungardy, p. 9.

2 Ibid. p. 9.

3 Ibid. p. 10.

4 Ibid. p. 9, 10, 14, 27.

5 Ibid. p. 20, 15–16, 27.

6 Ibid. p. 18. The details of prisoners digging new pits is taken

from Bungardy's caption on the photograph of the latrines in use.

7 Scott, p. 85; Bungardy, p. 24, 29.

8 Ibid. p. 21. He noted that packets of cards were sold at the inflated price of 1 shilling each.

9 *Der Kamerad,* 3 isssues: 12 June 1915, 19 June 1915, 26 June 1915.

10 Bungardy, p. 29.

11 Ibid. p. 22–23.

12 Ibid. p. 24.

13 'History of the Camp', Court of Enquiry, PART 2, p. 10.

14 'Witness Statement of Johann Gerdes at First Enquiry', Court of Enquiry, PART 1; 'Witness Statement of Wilhelm Holmann at First Enquiry', Court of Enquiry, PART 1.

15 Transcript of an interview with Harold Tilley, p. 3–4. State Library of South Australia, OH 276.

16 'Offener Brief an Major Logan', *Der Kamerad,* 22 June 1915.

17 'Letter from Colonel Sandford to the Minister of Defence, dated 11 August 1915', Court of Enquiry, PART 4.

18 'Record of First Enquiry', Court of Enquiry, PART 1.

19 'Witness Statement of Captain Hawkes at First Enquiry', Court of Enquiry, PART 1; 'Judgement at First Enquiry', Court of Enquiry, PART 1.

20 'Letter to Captain Hawkes from the Deputy Assistant Adjutant General Fourth Military District, 23 August 1915', Court of Enquiry, PART 4.

21 'Letter to the American Consul-General from Walter Emde, 17 April 1915', Court of Enquiry, PART 3; 'Department of Defence Minute Paper to the Secretary of the Department of Defence from the Chief of General Staff – Colonel Hubert Foster, dated 11 February 1916', Court of Enquiry, PART 5.

22 Ibid.; 'Letter from the American Consul General to Senator Pearce, Defence Minister', 31 January, 1915, Court of Enquiry, PART 5; 'Translation of letter from the German Foreign Office to the United States Embassy', 22 September 1915', Court of Enquiry PART 5.

23 'Record of Second Enquiry', Court of Enquiry, PART 2.

24 'Lange evidence', Court of Enquiry, PART 1; 'Witness Statement of Ernst Baumann at Second Enquiry', Court of Enquiry, PART 1 'Witness Statement of Heinrich von Zulow at Second Enquiry', Court of Enquiry, PART 1.

25 Bungardy, p. 33 says 15 feet by 9 feet.

26 'Orders for the detention of Otto Brechlin, Fred Muller, Heinrich Prengl, Ralph Schmidt, August Haucke and Gustav Lange', 23 March 1915, Court of Enquiry, PART 6; 'Evidence of Captain Hawkes', Court of Enquiry, PART 1.

27 'Judgment of Second Enquiry', Court of Enquiry, PART 2.

28 'Witness Statement of Captain Hawkes at Second Enquiry', Court of Enquiry, PART 1; 'Evidence of Captain Strycker', Court of Enquiry, PART 1.

29 'Witness Statement of Fritz Schroeder at Second Enquiry', Court of Enquiry, PART 1; 'Witness Statement of Captain Hawkes at Second Enquiry', Court of Enquiry, PART 1.

30 'Wilhelm Henry Matzelt's Witness Statement at Second Enquiry', Court of Enquiry, PART 1.

31 Mecke Beyer, whose name does not appear on either of the nominal rolls relating to Torrens Island Camp, is potentially another name for Albert Mick, who is noted as being sent to Parkside Asylum on the first nominal roll. Nominal roll of prisoners of war interned at Torrens Island concentration camp 1915, NAA: D2286, VOLUME 1, 'Witness Statement of Bernhard Wandert at Second Enquiry', Court of Enquiry, PART 1; 'Witness Statement of George Paul Fischer at Second Enquiry', Court of Enquiry, PART 1; 'Witness Statement of Hans Korth at Second Enquiry', Court of Enquiry, PART 1.

32 'Judgment of Second Enquiry', Court of Enquiry, PART 2.

33 Ibid.

34 Ibid.

35 'Letter to the Commonwealth Statistician from Captain Hawkes, 17 August 1916', Court of Enquiry, PART 5; HAWKES George Edward, NAA: B2455, HAWKES, G.E.

36 'Letter to the United States Ambassador from Sir Edward Grey, 2 December 1915', Court of Enquiry, PART 5; Prisoners of War – Torrens Island, Governor General, Governor General's correspondence relating to the war of 1914–1918 ['War Files], NAA: A11803, 1918/89/953.

Paul Dubotzki Nadine Helmi and Gerhard Fischer, *The Enemy at Home: German Internees in World War I Australia,* Sydney: UNSW Press, 2011, p. 7–15; personal communications to authors by Franz Streibl of Dorfen; NAA: D2286, Nominal roll of prisoners of war interned at Torrens Island concentration camp 1915.

**Frank Bungardy** *The Kadina and Wallaroo Times* (SA: 1888–1954), Wednesday 2 August 1911, p. 2; 'Bungardy Defeats Nathan', *Advertiser* (Adelaide, SA: 1889–1931), Tuesday 12 September 1911, p. 11; Bungardy, Frank, 'Frank W. Bungardy narrative of events at Torrens Island Internment Camp, 1915 and Holsworthy Internment Camp, 1915–ca. 1919', State Library of NSW, MLMSS 261/Box 2/Item 15, p. 3–4; NAA: D2375, VON BUNGARDY FRANZ WERNER; NAA: MP1565/2 List of Prisoners of War Captured and Interned in Australia.

**Der Kamerad** *Der Kamerad. Wochenschrift der Kriegsgefangenen auf Torrens Island, S. Australien*, edited by W. Emde, issue 1, 12 June 1915; issue 2, 19 June 1915; issue 3, 26 June 1915. State Library of South Australia.

**George Edward Hawkes** Service Record of George Edward Hawkes, NAA: B2455, Hawkes, G.E.

## 5. After Torrens Island

1 Morton, p. 104.

2 Fischer, *Enemy Aliens*, p. 247.

3 Ibid. p. 231–232.

4 Alan Foskett, 'The Molonglo internment Camp', http://www.m2cms.com.au/uploaded/18/The%20Molonglo%20internment%20Camp%20final.pdf; Fischer, *Enemy Aliens*, p. 270–271.

5 Fischer, 'Integration', p. 11.

6 Williams, p. 6, 10.

7 *Register*, 31 August 1917, p. 5.

8 *Advertiser*, 6 July 1916, p. 8.

9 Ibid. p. 8.

10 *Mail*, 18 August 1917, p. 1; *Register,* 4 September 1916, p. 5.

11 G. Grainger, 'Vaughan, Crawford (1874–1947)', Australian Dictionary of Biography, http://adb.anu.edu.au/biography/vaughan-crawford-8909/text15651, accessed 12 December 2013; *Advertiser,* 12 June 1917, p. 4; Lodewyckx, p. 237.

12 Ibid.

13 Rev John Blacket, letter, *Register*, 7 May 1918.

14 Manning.

15 Fischer, 'Integration', p. 11.

16 Joan Hancock and Eric Richards, 'Muecke, Hugo Carl Emil (1842–1929)', Australian Dictionary of Biography, http://adb.anu.edu.au/biography/muecke-hugo-carl-emil-7674/text13427, accessed 12 December 2013.

17 Morton, p. 295–296.

18 Fischer, p. 285, 290, 302; Morton, p. 326.

19 Morton, p. 326; Fischer, p. 301–302.

**Bulgarians** 'Arrest of Bulgarians. Causes Labour Shortage Smelters. Enemy Subjects Taken to Adelaide', *Port Pirie Recorder and North Western Mail*, 15 November 1915, p. 4; *House of Representatives. Official Hansard*. No. 20, 1916, 18 May 1917, p. 7981; 'The Released Bulgarians. Men indignant. Minister for Defence communicated with. Explanation Tendered'. *Port Pirie Recorder and North Western Mail*, 20 May 1916, p. 3.

**The Dechert Brothers** Germans and Public Employ. Disloyalty of the Decherts. Thousands of Pounds Drawn from British Crown', *Mail* 14 October 1916, p. 5; NAA: MP1565/2, List of Prisoners of War Captured and Interned in Australia; Death Notices, *Advertiser*, 30 December 1926, p. 8.

**Leopold Ebner** NAA: D1915, SA434, Ebner, Leopold – permission to return to Australia – repatriated Austrian.

**Carl Ernst** NAA: D1915 SA262, Ernst, Carl – Pyap, near Loxton, SA – disloyalty and internment.

**Hermann Carl Goers** Ian Harmstorf, 'World War I: When Torrens Island was a Concentration Camp. A Dark Chapter in South Australia's History', http://www.thegermanclub.com.au/about-us/german-history-in-SA.php#WWITheGermans; letter written Liverpool 7 August 1918 by Goers to Miss Nora Goers (daughter), NAA: D1915 SA15119, GOERS, Hermann Carl; NAA: MP1565/2 WHOLE SERIES List of Prisoners of War Captured and Interned in Australia; Intelligence summary on Hermann Carl Goers, p. 2, NAA: D1915, SA 15119.

**Karl Wilhelm Lude** NAA: A11928/3723, Lude, WK – Naturalisation certificate; NAA: BP4/3, GERMAN LUDE K W, Lude, Karl Wilhelm – Nationality: German – Alien Registration Certificate.

**John Tossold** NAA: A435 1946/4/4178, TOSOLD John – born 31 May 1870 – Stateless; NAA: B2455 TOSOLD JOHN.

**Heinrich von Zülow** NAA: A1 1919/14799 Heinrich Ernst Augustus Wilhelm Von Zulow, Naturalisation.

# Bibliography

## Primary Sources

### Archival and Library holdings

#### Mitchell Library, State Library of New South Wales (SLNSW)

Various items from the collection: MLMSS 261, Papers of enemy aliens interned in Australia, 1914–1919. (Includes in Box 2, item 15, Frank W. Bungardy narrative of events at Torrens Island Internment Camp, 1915 and Holsworthy Internment Camp, 1915–ca. 1919.)

#### National Archives of Australia (NAA)

Items from the following series:

A367 C18000 Part 1, War Internees and Deportees 1914–1919.

A435, Class 4 correspondence files relating to naturalisation.

A11919, Migrant Selection Documents for Displaced Persons who travelled to Australia per General Black departing Naples 16 November 1949.

B78, Alien registration documents.

B2455, First Australian Imperial Force Personnel Dossiers, 1914–1920.

BP4/3, Alien registration forms, alphabetical series by nationality.

D1915, Investigation case files, single number series with 'SA' (South Australia) prefix.

D2286, Nominal roll of prisoners of war interned at Torrens Island concentration camp 1915.

D2375, Index cards to Prisoners-of-War (internees), 4th Military District, alphabetical series.

D3597, Album of identification *photographs* of enemy aliens (civilian and prisoner of war) interned at Liverpool Camp, NSW during World War I (with index).

MP367/1 General correspondence files.

MP367/1, 567/3/2202, Captain G.E. Hawkes, 77th Infantry – Court of Enquiry – Torrens Island Concentration Camp. 6 parts.

MP1565/2 WHOLE SERIES List of prisoners of War Captured and Interned in Australia.

#### State Library of South Australia (SLSA)

*Der Kamerad. Wochenschrift der Kriegsgefangenen auf Torrens Island, S. Australien, herausgegeben v. W. Emde*, 3 isssues: 12 June 1915, 19 June 1915, 26 June 1915.

Letters from Wilhelm Reinhard, D Piece (Archival) D 7027(L).

Transcript of an interview with Harold Tilley, p. 3–4. Oral history collection, OH 276.

### Published primary sources

Parliamentary Debates South Australia (Hansard).

Samuels, Edward, *An Illustrated Diary of Australian Internment Camps,* Sydney: Tyrell's, 1919.

Trojan, Martin, *Hinter Stein und Stacheldraht. Australische Schattenbilder,* Bremen: Carl Schünemann n. d., 1922.

Trove digitised newspapers, http://trove.nla.gov.au/newspaper.

## Secondary Sources


*Australian Dictionary of Biography*, National Centre of Biography, Australian National University, http://adb.anu.edu.au/.

Beaumont, Joan, Ilma Martinuzzi O'Brien, Mathew Trinca (eds.), *Under Suspicion: Citizenship and Internment in Australia during the Second World War*, Canberra: National Museum of Australia Press, 2008.

Day, David, *Andrew Fisher: Prime Minister of Australia,* Sydney: HarperCollins, 2008.

Fischer, Gerhard, *Enemy Aliens: Internment and the Homefront Experience in Australia 1914–1920*, Brisbane: University of Queensland Press, 1989.

Fischer, Gerhard, 'Integration, "Negative Integration", Disintegration: The Destruction of the German-Australian Community during the First World War', in Saunders, Kay, and Roger Daniels (ed.), *Alien Justice: Wartime Internment in Australia and North America*, Brisbane: UQP, 2000.

Harmstorf, Ian, 'Guests or Fellow-Countrymen. A Study in Assimilation. An Aspect of the German Community in South Australia 1836–1918', doctoral thesis, Flinders University, 1987.

Harmstorf, Ian, 'When Torrens Island was a Concentration Camp', *Sunday Mail,* 2 September 1979, p. 2, 56.

Harmstorf, Ian, 'World War I: When Torrens Island was a Concentration Camp. A Dark Chapter in South Australia's History', http://www.thegermanclub.com.au/about-us/german-history-in-SA.php#WWITheGermans.

Harmstorf, Ian and Michael Cigler (eds.), *The Germans in Australia*, Melbourne: AE Press, 1985.

Helmi, Nadine, and Gerhard Fischer, *The Enemy at Home: German Internees in World War I Australia*, Sydney: UNSW Press, 2011.

Jupp, James (ed.), *The Australian People. An Encyclopedia of the Nation, Its People and Their Origins*, Cambridge: Cambridge University Press, 2001.

Lodewyckx, Augustin, *Die Deutschen in Australien*, Stuttgart: Ausland und Heimat Verlagsgesellschaft, 1932.

Manning, Geoffrey H., 'World War I and the Fate of German Place Names', in 'Geoff Manning's Insight into South Australian History', http://www.geoffmanning.net.au/html/german-placenames.html.

McKernan, Michael, *The Australian People and the Great War,* Melbourne: Nelson, 1980.

Monteath, Peter (ed.), *Germans: Travellers, Settlers and Their Descendants in South Australia*, Adelaide: Wakefield Press, 2011.

Morton, Richard James, 'The Enemy Within the Gates: The Internment of Australian Citizens during the Great War', doctoral thesis, La Trobe University, 1990.

Paech, David, *Persecution, Detention and Internment of Lutherans in South Australia in Two World Wars: A Dark Spot in Australia's Centenary of Federation*, Adelaide: David O. Paech, 2001.

Scott, Ernest, *Australia During the War*. Volume IX of The Official History of Australia in the War of 1914–1918, 7th ed., Sydney: Angus & Robertson, 1941.

Tampke, Jürgen, *Australia, Willkommen: A History of the Germans in Australia*, Sydney: UNSW Press, 1990.

Tampke, Jürgen, *The Germans in Australia*, Melbourne: Cambridge University Press, 2006.

Voigt, Johannes H., *Australia-Germany: Two Hundred Years of Contacts, Relations and Connections*, Bonn: Inter Nationes, 1987.

Weiss, Johann Peter, *It Wasn't Really Necessary. Internment in Australia with Emphasis on the Second World War,* Adelaide: the author, 2003.

Williams, John F., *German Anzacs and the First World War*, Sydney: UNSW Press, 2003.

When it was established in 1986, South Australia's Migration Museum was the first museum of migration history in the world. Over the decades since then, it has established a reputation for ground-breaking exhibitions and public programs, and continues to lead in its commitment to community engagement. The Migration Museum is a museum of History SA, the statutory body responsible for the preservation, research and interpretation of South Australia's history. This was also a ground-breaking body when established and is unique in its commitment to supporting history throughout the state.

The exhibition *Interned: Torrens Island, 1914–1915*, was presented at the Migration Museum from 11 October 2014 to 16 August 2015.

ULRICH MEIER
EBNER
EMDE